The Second Boo

COTSW

RAMBLES

25 Short Walks In The Finest Part Of The Cotswolds

Harry Hargreaves

Published by
Thornhill Press
24 Moorend Road
Cheltenham

AUTHOR'S NOTE

As we have rambled in the Cotswolds, my companions and I felt that the richness of this rambling required that it should be recorded for others in this second book, which sets out twenty-five new walks.

These short walks are in no way inferior to the ones in the first book; indeed, we are certain that as a result of the greater experience, this book will be found to be no less interesting.

I must repeat the acknowledgements which I made in the first book.

I am appreciative of all the people and the organisations who, by their activities in keeping open and conserving the countryside have helped to make possible the production of this book. Special mention must be made of the Cotswold Wardens, the Ramblers' Association, the Common Open Spaces and Footpaths Preservation Society, the National Trust and the Countryside Commission. My thanks are due to the Footpaths Section of the Gloucestershire County Council for their help in the definition of Rights of Way and in communicating with landowners to get obstructions removed.

My pleasure in walking with the Evesham Ramblers has been a constant stimulus to the production of these books.

My friend Peter Price is responsible for producing the excellent map on the back of this book.

Finally, all those interested in the preparation of this book are very appreciative of those farmers who have been helpful in removing obstructions and have co-operated in the clearance of footpaths.

HARRY HARGREAVES

The Country Code

Please remember as you walk throughout the countryside to respect the privacy and livelihood of those who live in the country.

The Country Code asks you to:-

1. Guard against all risks of fires.
2. Fasten all gates.
3. Keep dogs under proper control.
4. Keep to paths across farmland.
5. Avoid damaging fences, hedges, and walls.
6. Leave no litter.
7. Safeguard water supplies.
8. Protect wildlife, plants and trees.
9. Go carefully on country roads.
10. Respect the life of the countryside.

INTRODUCTION

This book contains rambles a few of which could be done in a morning or an afternoon or an evening. But allow more than this as invariably there are delays arising from say a search for a stile, a gate or a path and for a linger because of some point of special interest. Whilst they are described as short walks they should not be thought of as gentle strolls. The shortest walk is 2½ miles and the longest 11. Most of them are between 5 and 7 miles. If a walk is over 5 miles then, if it is being done for the first time, then allow a full day.

The rambles are in that part of the Cotswolds between Broadway in the north and Cirencester in the south. Bredon is not strictly in the Cotswolds, but is so near and so lovely a walk, it had to be included.

It is hoped that the narrative of each ramble is so detailed that it is not necessary to use a map. However, at the beginning of each ramble is a copy of the Ordnance Map. These are on the 1:50,000 scale (Approx. 1¼" to the mile). This will enable the rambler to see the ramble in outline and, if the narrative is departed from, it should help to get back to the right way.

The Ordnance Map number for the area on the 1:50,000 scale is stated at the beginning of each ramble. This will be of interest to the rambler who wishes to relate his walking to the surrounding country.

It is stating the obvious to say: make sure you get to the right starting point: otherwise everything is wrong.

At the beginning of each ramble a place is named which is related by number to the map on the back cover. From this named place a description is given of how to get to the starting point.

Each ramble starts and finishes at the same place.

INDEX

RAMBLE ONE

BROADWAY and WILLERSLEY

A walk designed around these villages so as to keep away from the roads. Distance 5 miles. Map 150 in the 1/50,000 series. Starting point grid reference 094376 Village of Broadway. The start is from the Swan Hotel in Broadway.

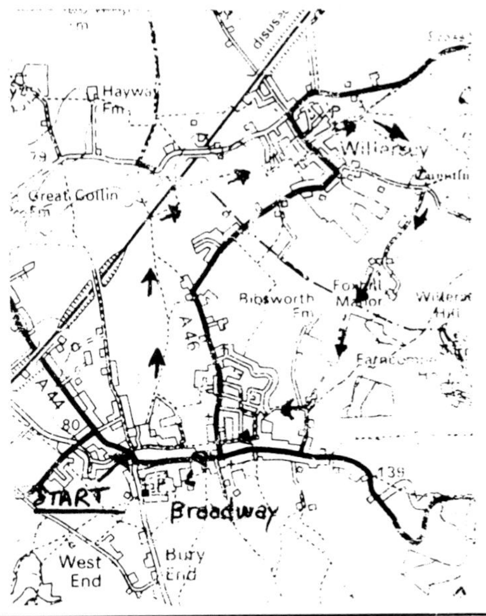

Facing the hotel, go down the road immediately to the left of the Swan Hotel car park. In 45 yards, go along the first road on the left – Walnut Close. At the end of this close, bear right and take the path indicated by the footpath signpost. Follow this path to a kissing gate, and turn left to a point about 6 yards before it enters a field. Here, take a path on the right and follow a hedge which is on the left to a bridge over a ditch. Cross this and continue in the same direction to a facing wooden kissing gate. (If there are growing crops in this field, then after crossing the bridge, turn left and, at the facing hedge, turn right. This hedge forms an arc and this should be followed to where the arc straightens out. At this point, there is the kissing gate referred to above.)

Go through the kissing gate and walk with a hedge on the left. Cross into the next field and continue with a fence on the left to a gateway. Go through and immediately turn right and follow the hedge on the right to a wide gap. Cross the field in the same direction to another gap. Pass through and walk with the ditch on the right to a gate. Go through the gate into the next field. The old railway (no lines) is 40 yards ahead, but do not go towards it but turn immediately right and arrive at the facing hedge about 100 yards from the railway on the left. Turn left and keep the hedge on the right for about 100 yards and then turn right over the footbridge to pass into the adjacent field. Follow the hedge and old railway on the left and cross a ditch and field so as to pass to the right of some farm buildings. Keep the hedge on the left to the outskirts of Willersey.

Turn right into the roadway by Hays Close and first left along the back of Hays Close. This path goes to the left of the village hall. In any case, once in Willersey, go to the church with the tower, i.e. first left on the main road, and then first right.

Enter the churchyard and follow the path to the left. Go through the kissing gate on the left and follow the wall then the hedge on the right to the end of the field. Go over the stile into the next field. Follow the hedge on the left to an orchard and cross a stile and continue ahead up the next field with a hedge on the left. About 30 yards before the end of the orchard, turn right to a gate which gives access to the road. Cross the road and go up the road opposite.

After passing through a security gate, go along a road bearing right to follow the footpath waymarkings. Pass through the car park of Securicor and proceed with a hedge on the right to go through the first gateway on the right with a footpath waymarking. In this field, bear left to pass to the left of a large ash tree. Continue in the same direction to a stile and cross a field to a stone bridge across a ditch. Continue with a hedge on the left to an orchard. Continue through the orchard near a fence and hedge to a stile. Cross the stile and proceed ahead to the wooden fence. Turn right and follow the wooden fence to a gate on the left with a blue bridleway sign. Here, bear right to a small gate and continue to a second small gate which gives access to the road.

Cross this road and go down the road opposite. In about 30 yards leave the metal road and go over a stile on the left and follow the hedge on the left to a stile. Cross it and follow the path to the road. Cross the road and go down the path opposite.

At the next road, turn left (Orchard Avenue) and then, at the T junction turn right. This leads to the A46. Cross and turn left and in about 10 yards go over a stone stile on the right and take the track which leads to the Swan Hotel and the beginning and end of the walk.

BROADWAY

A nature trail and some fine views when descending to Broadway
Distance 4 miles Map 150 in the 1:500000 series.
Starting point map re. 120368 – the Fish Hill Picnic Site.

To get to the starting point from Broadway take the A44 up Fish Hill. About 300 yards over the brow of the hill take the first turn on the left signposted to Chipping Camden. The picnic site is almost immediately on the left. Cars may be parked here.

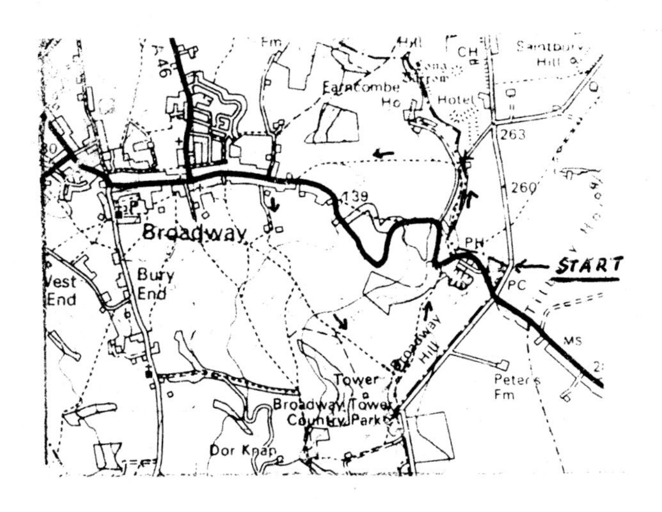

Walk in the picnic site due west for about 150 yards to a topograph which is the actual starting point of the walk. Immediately in front will be seen a wooden signpost: follow the Woodland Walk sign to a wood. About 50 yards in the wood, descend some steps on the left to a track: turn right. Follow the red top posts to a "fossil notice": continue ahead up some steps in the bank.

From the top of the steps go forward for 10yards. Then turn right and follow the definite footpath. Descend some steps and go over a stile on to the road.

Cross the road and go over the stile with a footpath signpost. Walk northwards so as to descend with the fence to the right. Veer away from the fence so as to be 100 yards to the left of it on arriving at the facing hedge, where there is a stile.

Having crossed the stile continue the descent in the same direction making for a point where a hedge from the right makes a junction with a hedge continuing the line of descent. Walk on with this latter hedge on the right to a gate: pass through and follow the track to an open field and then continue with a hedge and fence on the left to another gate. Go through the small gate on the left and over the stile fence immediately in front. (This is an awkward fence at the time of writing, but it is hoped to get a proper stile.) Continue with the fence on the right to the main road, A44.

Turn right. In 250 yards, take a footpath on the left signposted Broadway Tower. Ascend the hill by the Cotswold Way signs (white dot with a yellow arrow) to Broadway Tower.

Go to the left of the Tower and pass through a gate on the left. Now follow the footpath with a wall on the right. Where the wall ends Cotswold Way signs on posts will be seen ahead: follow these and continue to a gate. Pass through into a wood. In a few yards the track forks; follow the Cotswold Way signs to the road A44. Cross the road to the topograph which will be seen as the road is crossed and thus ends the walk where it began.

RAMBLE 3

BROADWAY, BUCKLAND, LAVERTON, STANTON

Surely 4 of the finest villages in the Cotswolds
Map OS 150 in the 1: 50000 series
Starting point grid ref. 100378 Broadway: the car park off the A46. Distance 8 miles.

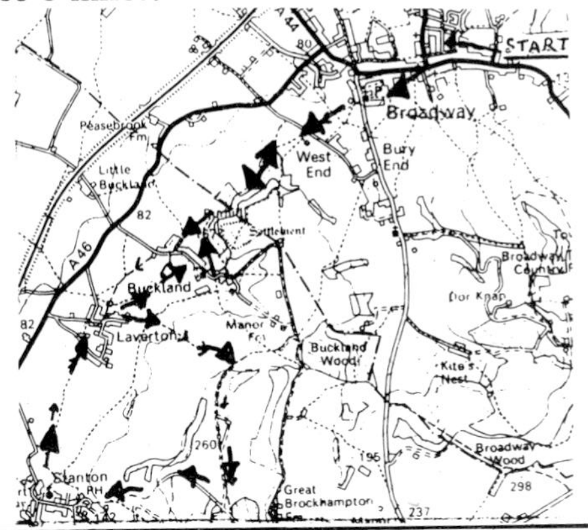

On leaving the car park, at the A46, turn left to the A44. Turn right. In about 100 yards, turn left along a footpath, signposted to the church, opposite the Horse & Hounds Inn. In about 60 yards, on entering a field, turn right and go over the stile. Follow the fence on the right. The fence is followed by a wall at the end of which turn left for about 15 yards and go over the stile on the right. Go ahead to a farm road. Turn left.

In about 100 yards, cross the green on the right to a kissing gate. Go through and follow the track through some rough ground and woodland. On coming into the open continue ahead and pass through a kissing gate on to a metalled track with houses on the left, to the road.

Cross this and go down the track opposite which is waymarked Cotswold Way. Follow the Cotswold Way signs. The path crosses a tiny stream and continues ahead to the road.

Cross the road and go over the stile which is on the left hand side of a gate. This is now departing from the Cotswold Way. Ascend to the wood on the left making for a point about 35 yards from the right hand end of the wood. Go over the stile, with a public footpath waymark, into the wood. Continue ahead along the track with a fence on the right for about 50 yards. Go straight on with the main part of the wood on the left for about another 150 yards to a stile on the right with a waymark. Go over and continue ahead along the rising ground. At another waymark, continue ahead along a narrow track with a fence on the right.

On coming out of the narrow track, continue ahead with a fence on the right and some scrubland on the left for about 200 yards to a gate and go over the waymarked stile on the right. Here bear right in accordance with the waymarked sign on a post in the wire fence and follow the definite track around the hill 15 yards below the fence on the left. Where the path may fork, keep to the right one which follows the contour of the hill. Ascend to a stile with a waymark. Cross this and go between two trees with waymarks and descend to another stile alongside a fence. Now follow a sequence of stiles passing over a small stream and through a kissing gate into a metalled track. Go past the rectory, which is on the left, to the road in Buckland.

Turn right. In about 150 yards there is a small open space on the left. Take the bridleway straight ahead. Follow the clear track to Laverton. In Laverton turn left and walk to the end of the village and pass through a gate with a stile on the right.

Bear right to a sunken track. Follow this to a gate which pass through and still follow the definite track. At one point the track opens out and levels. Continue ahead and ascend to a definite track with a number of fine beeches and a Cotswold Way sign. Turn right. Go through a gate and continue along the same definite track passing to the right of Laverton Hill Barn about 70 yards away. In about 600 yards pass through a gate and continue along the definite track to a T junction with another definite track.

Turn right and go through a gate and proceed along the descending track. In the course of the descent do not follow the track as it goes to the left along the contour of the hill, but continue descending to arrive at the Mount Inn in Stanton. Descend to the village and continue ahead down the street. At the village cross, turn right to the church. Go into the churchyard and pass to the right of the church. Take a narrow track on the right between walls. Do not follow the narrow track when it turns left, but go over the stile in front to enter a field. Turn left. Follow the hedge on the left to a stile at a point where the hedge goes to the right and then left.

Go over the stile and follow the hedge which is on the right. Pass over a stile into the next field and continue to follow the hedge which is on the right. Pass into another field and go ahead with the hedge still on the right. At the end of this field, follow the hedge as it turns left. In 15 yards, go over the stone stile on the right and follow the hedge which is on the left. At the end of this field go over the stile and straight ahead over a second stile. Continue ahead with a hedge now on the right. At the corner of the field turn left for a few yards and pass over a stile into the road. Turn left. In about 100 yards, pass over a stile on the right which is to the left of a drive to a large house. Pass over an iron fence into a field. Follow the hedge which is on the right and pass through a gate into another field. Continue ahead to another stile. Cross and go through a private garden by keeping close to the right hand boundary.

At the road in Laverton, turn right and continue to a point where there is a road on the right. Immediately past this road, take the walled track on the left.

In just over 100 yards where the wall on the left finishes go through a gate on the right. (The gate is opposite a signposted footpath on the left). Bear left diagonally across the field and walk to the right of an electricity pole in mid-field to a stile. Go over the stile and follow the hedge which is on the left. Follow this hedge as it makes a curve to the right in roughly the shape of a horseshoe. At the apex of the horseshoe there is a gate. (It is the first gate since the stile.) Go through and follow the hedge which is on the right round the headland of the field to a wooden fence. Go over this wooden fence and continue ahead so as to walk with a line of conifers on the left and a line of hazel bushes on the right. At the end of the conifers go through the wooden fence on the left into a field. Walk diagonally right to the hedge about 30 yards away so as to. arrive at a gate in the hedge about 30 yards from the wooden fence Pass through the gate into the road in Buckland.

Turn right. At almost the end of the village, after the road has completed an S curve, and where it begins to ascend and bears right leave the road to follow the waymark on the corner of the building on the left. (The waymark is not very obvious, but if it is missed, then identify the route by the building about 30 yards before a house called Burhill.)

Climb up the slope and in 30 yards go over a stile. Bear left and follow the definite track ascending over the waymarked stiles to an open field. Go ahead in the same direction with the fence on the right about 15 yards away. Go over a knoll. On descending, veer left away from the fence to a stile in the facing fence. Follow the fence on the right to a waymarked stile. Now follow the waymarks through the wood for about ½ mile. Leave the wood by a stile into a field and descend to the stile in the bottom right hand corner of the field. Cross the road to the stile and gate on the opposite side. Now follow the track over a bridge and tiny stream and rise to the road. Cross and go up the metalled track opposite with houses on the right. Go through a gate and continue ahead. Descend along the track as is passes into a thicket. Pass through the thicket and go through a wicket gate. Proceed ahead through a kissing gate on to a green. Veer left and go over a farm road leaving some farm buildings to the left. Immediately past the farm buildings, go over a stile into a field. Now follow the left hand boundary of the field to a stile in the corner. Go over and turn left and in 50 yards come to the A44 in Broadway. Here turn right and then left along the Leamington Road to the public car park from where the walk started.

STANWAY, WOOD STANWAY, HAILES, BECKBURY CAMP

Map 150 in the 1: 50000 series
Starting point grid ref. 061322 on the B4077 road about 200 yards south of the village of Stanway. Distance 6 miles.

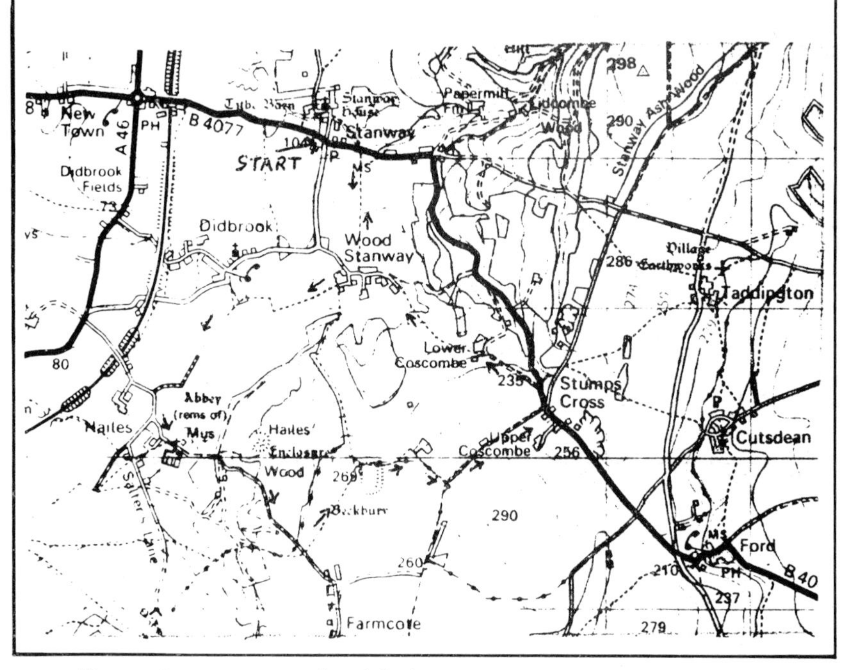

From the cross roads with St George & the Dragon monument on the left, walk up the road for 250 yards. Take the signposted public footpath on the right and follow it to Wood Stanway.

At the road, turn right and take the first road on the left. Follow the road round to a gate. Go through into the field and follow the hedge which is on the right tot he corner of the field. Go into the next field and walk so as to veer away from the hedge on the right to arrive about 100 yards from it at a facing hedge. Go through the gate and continue straight ahead at the bottom of the slope on the left to a gate in the facing hedge. Pass into the next field, turn right and follow the hedge which is on the right to the corner. Turn left and continue to follow a hedge on the right and pass an orchard which is on the right to a facing hedge. Go over the stile and continue to follow the hedge which is on the right to a definite track. Follow this round to the right to the road.

Turn left. When the road forks, go to the left and continue past Hailes Abbey. This ruin is under the National Trust. The Abbey was founded in 1246 by Richard, Earl of Cornwall, in fulfilment of a vow made on escaping from a shipwreck on the Scillies, and delivered to the Cistercian Order of Monks. In 1270 the monks were presented by Edmund, second Earl of Cornwall with a phial containing the famous "Blood of Hailes" which, until the Dissolution of the Monasteries in 1539 was the most revered object of the Abbey, and the cynosure of countless pilgrims. Its authenticity had been guaranteed by the Patriarch of Jerusalem (later Pope Urban IV). The church on the other side of the road was built c.1130.

Ascend up the definite track. Avoid the road on the right which leads to a fruit farm. Almost at the top of the ascent, just before the hamlet of North Farmcote, take the footpath on the left signposted Beckbury Camp which is an Ancient British Camp.

Go over the stile, and proceed in the direction indicated by the signpost (compass bearing 39°). Ascend through 2 waymarked gates towards the monument. Pass a waymarked post and continue to the foot of the escarpment. Now climb up to the monument.

From the monument, go through the waymarked gate and walk with a wall and fence on the left. This is now inside the earthworks of Beckbury Camp. There is a magnificent view of the Vale of Evesham and Bredon Hill on the left. Walk over 2 fields to the corner of the second field. Turn right and with a stone wall on the left, proceed for about 300 yards and, just before a small plantation ahead, go through a gate on the left. Turn right and follow a wall which is on the right to a track which is Campden Lane. Turn left and in ½ mile, the main road is reached at Stumps Cross (note the Stump!).

Turn down the road, and in just over 100 yards take a track on the left signposted Wood Stanway. Now follow the Cotswold waymark signs through Lower Corscombe farm all the way to Wood Stanway.

In the hamlet, turn right along a signposted track in the reverse direction to that taken at the beginning of the walk. At the road, turn left to the start of the walk.

RAMBLE 5

BREDON

Map OS in the 1:50000 series

Starting point grid ref. 941378 Village of Westmancote

Distance 6 miles

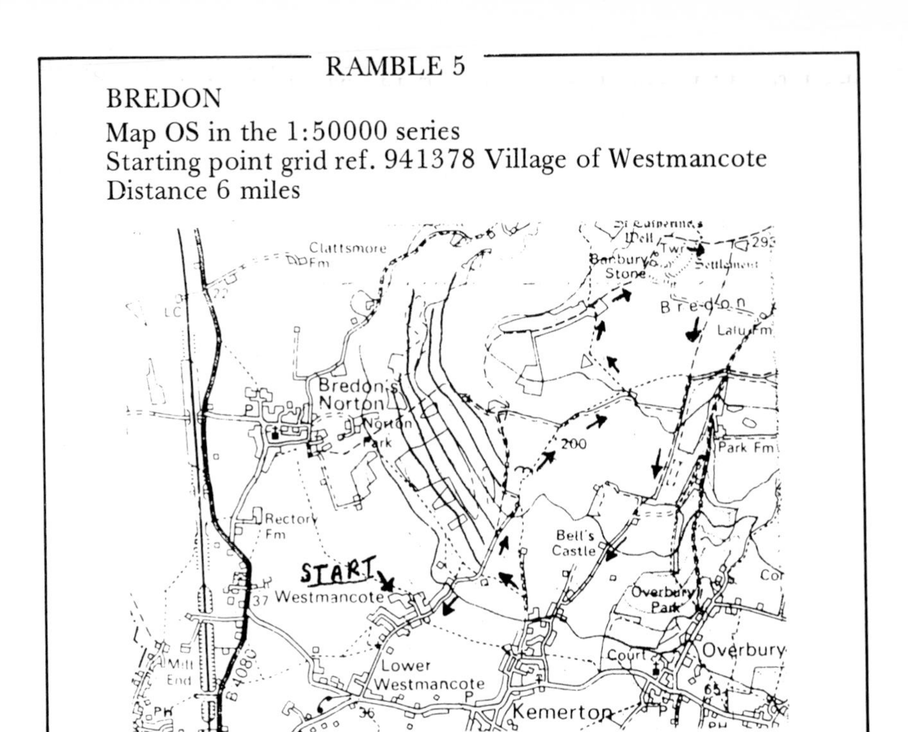

To get to Westmancote :–

From Evesham – Take the Cheltenahm road A435(T) and in 7 miles turn right at the Beckford Inn. Go through the village of Beckford and follow the road through the villages of Overbury and Kemerton. After passing through Kemerton, continue to a junction of roads and take the road on the right at Lower Westmancote. Go ahead for ¼ mile to Westmancote.

From Tewkesbury – Take the B4080 towards the village of Bredon, leave Bredon by the B4079 and in about 350 yards where the main road turns right, keep left to Lower Westmancote. At the junction of roads take the second on the left to Westmancote.

This is the start of the ramble.

Go on up the road and continue ascending when it becomes a very rough road. At a fork, bear right through a gateway and up a sunken pathway. At a second fork bear right again, the track being between hedges. Enter a gated field, proceed alongside a fence on the left for 100 yards and then bear right to follow the hedge on the left which runs between two fields. The hedge is intermittent and does not form a definite barrier. Do not go into the field on the left, but go north-east uphill with the intermittent hedge on the left. The track becomes a definite bridleway going uphill. Go through the gate at the junction of rail-fence and wall and continue with wall on left. The wall is succeeded by a fence and hedge still on the left. Pass through the gate.

The unoccupied buildings of Sundial Farm are 50 yards ahead. The Sundial has gone but its face can be seen on the gable facing south.

Go over the stile 35 yards beyond the gate and continue with the wall on the left past a copse on the left, towards the line of trees ahead. Here cross a stile and turn right, walking now with the narrow strip of trees on the left and wire fence on the right for 250 yards. At some fir trees bear left (do not take the sharp left descending cutting), then right – still ascending. Pass through a gate in a wall into a field and walk with the wall on the left to the tower on the top of Bredon Hill.

Bear left and continue along the rim of the hill with a wall on the left. The wall swings to the right and then passes through a gate in a wire fence. Go ahead with the wall on the left to a gate with a fir copse on the other side. Do not pass through the gate, but turn right and descend gently with the wall on the left. Pass through a gate in a wall and then in 200 yards, pass through a facing gate in a fence. Go through the next facing gate in a wall. Continue descent with a wall on the left, through another gate in a wall and yet another in a further 200 yards.

Pass an old quarry on the right and go through a gate. Pass through 100 yards of wood on a track leading to barns on the left and a metalled road. This descends quite steeply past Bell's Castle: a private house said to have been built by a former seaman and smuggler.

Continue down, and after a right/left zig-zag, take the first metalled road on the right. In about 200 yards, where the road swings sharp left, turn sharp right and immediately cross the stile by the gate. Continue ascending up the rough track past a hedge on the left and turn left in front of the second hedge along a path with a wire fence on the left and the hedge on the right which takes you to the right of a cottage. At the metalled road in front of the cottage, turn left and descend into Westmancote along the route with which the walk commenced.

MICKLETON, HIDCOTE BOYCE, FOXCOTE,
HIDCOTE BARTRIM

A walk in pastoral country with Cotswold villages and hamlets and the National Trust gardens at Hidcote Bartrim.

Map OS 151 in the 1: 50000 series.
Starting point grid ref. 161435 Mickleton Church
Distance 7 miles

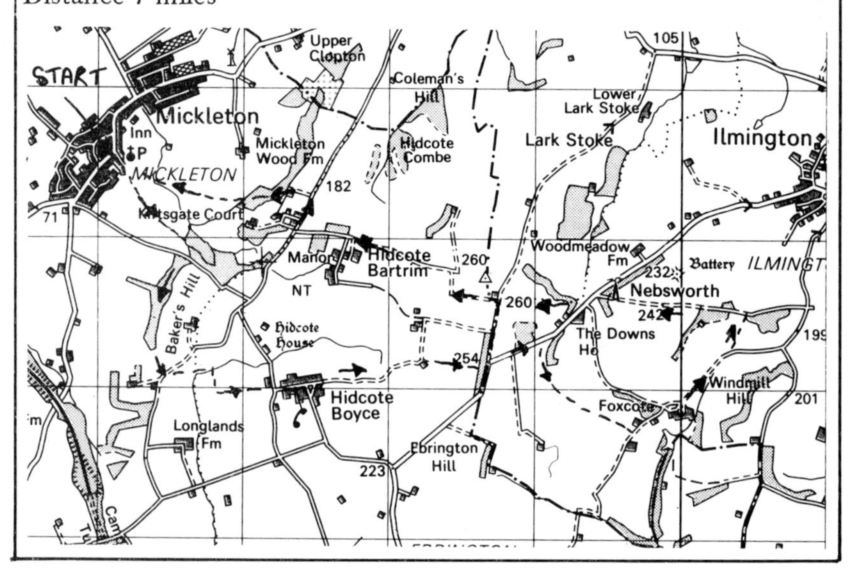

From the A46 take the lane to Mickleton church (a limited number of cars may be parked here). Pass the car park, bear left and in 10 yards, turn right up a grassy bank to a kissing gate into a field. Cross this field, keeping close to the hedge on the right and in 150 yards drop down to a gate. Cross a brook, then walk along a path through trees to a wicket gate. Pass through into a large field. Keeping the hedge about 10 yards on the left, cross the field to a kissing gate. Pass through and bear right up the slope to the top left hand corner of the field. Go through the gate on to the road.

Cross the road and climb the bank and go through a gate; turn right and walk round the edge of the field with a wood on the right. In about 200 yards, go through a wicket gate into the wood. Proceed along the path, parallel with the fence on the left, along Baker's Hill. (The path is lined with many fine, mature beech trees and there is a good view to the west.)

On coming out of the wood, continue in the same direction to a black barn and the entrance to Starveal Farm. Turn left at the barn and go straight across the farm road to follow alongside a hedge on the left for about 250 yards to a brook. Cross, turn left (marker post) and walk round the field headland with a hedge and small stream on the left to an iron gate; turn right and carry on round the same field with hedge on left, past a pylon. In 30 yards past the pylon turn left through a gateway and proceed for about 250 yards along a cart track till the road is reached. Go up the road opposite into Hidcote Boyce village.

Where the road turns right, continue straight ahead up the track and enter a field. After about 350 yards, the track enters another field with a boundary hedge. Ascend with this hedge about 20 yards to the right till a grassy disused quarry is reached. Keep immediately to the left of the quarry and a large stone barn and make for a gateway in a stone wall about 150 yards ahead from the barn; pass through this gateway with a stone wall on the left and carry on for 350 yards to the road.

Go up the opposite and straight road for about 500 yards and where the road bends to the left, take the bridleway (sign on gate-post) on the right and, with a coppice alongside on the left, walk for about 400 yards. Where the coppice ends, carry straight on, first with a wall and then a hedge on the right, over a stile and into a field to Foxcote Farm some 250 yards in front.

At the farm, turn left to Foxcote House. Opposite the main entrance, bear left along the road and in 500 yards a fairly prominent stone barn (Dunstall Building) will be seen on the left about 300 yards above the road. Where the road takes a slight bend to the right, leave the road and cross a stile in the left hand fence and ascend the hill keeping close to a hedge which is on the right. At the top of this ascent turn left on a bridle way (Pig Lane).

Go along Pig Lane for about ½ mile, passing the radar/TV masts at Nebworth to a road. Turn left and in 50 yards, take the gate on the right (footpath signpost). Proceed half left up the field and pass through a wicket gate. Continue up the slope for 25 yards and then turn right and follow round the edge of the field with a stone wall and wire fence on the right. Continue ahead over a minor road/track past a booster station and thence along the track for about a mile to the National Trust car park of Hidcote Manor.

Continue ahead along the road to a T junction; then cross to the signpost and go through the nearby gate in the wall. This gives access to parkland with Kiftsgate Court on the right. Descend, veering slightly left to pass through a gap in the bottom of the valley. Continue ahead with a stream on the left. Pass through several gates with waymark signs. On entering the field before Mickleton Church, bear slightly right and then turn left round the new cemetry and so down the lane to the church car park and into Mickleton.

RAMBLE 7

DOVERS HILL and CHIPPING CAMPDEN

A ridge walk along National Trust property and a pleasant circle round Chipping Campden.

Distance 6½ miles.
Map 151 in the 1: 50000 series
Starting point Grid ref. 137395 Dovers Hill National Trust car park: about 1½ miles west of Chipping Campden.

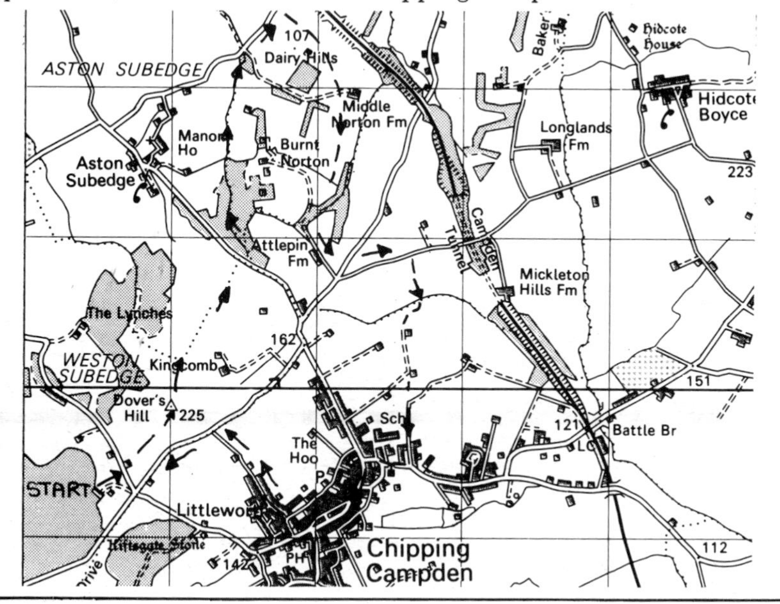

From the car park, pass through the kissing gate and follow the edge of the ridge with open country on the left and a boundary of trees and shrubs on the right. Continue ahead for 1 mile with fine views of the Vale of Evesham on the left, passing over two stiles, the second with a NT sign, to the road.

Cross road and go through the gate opposite to enter the wood. Follow the track on the left as indicated by a waymarked sign. On emerging from the wood by a gate, carry on downhill keeping close to the wood on the right for about 450 yards to a farm track on the bottom of the hill. Go through gate on right, over a small stream and in 20 yards, go left over a stile into a field. Continue ahead across the field with hedge and stream on the left. Pass into the next field over a stile and walk with the stream still on the left for 400 yards; go over a stile and small bridge to the road.

Turn right up the road for about 400 yards, and then take a bridle track on the right: in about 30 yards, pass through a gate, cross two fields with a hedge and ditch on the left to a gate. Pass through and bear righthanded to the corner of wood on right. Carry on over the field in the same direction, crossing a farm road to a gate in the corner of the field about 150 yards from the farm.

Pass through and carry on up the slope with hedge and ditch on left to a gate: go through and on in the same direction over a field to another gate (bridle-way marked) past 2 very old stone gate posts and in about 200 yards, to a further gate (bridle-way marked) at the edge of the wood.

Pass through the gate and along the green track with wood on left and farm road on right for 250 yards till the green track merges with the farm road. Carry on with farm building on the right to the road (B4081).

Cross the road and take the fork marked Hidcote Boyce. In about 550 yards at the bottom of a slight descent, go over a stile (waymarked) on the right into a field and walk on the foot-path for about 300 yards with hedge on left to a facing hedge and stream. Pass into next field over the stream at footbridge and walk diagonally right towards farm buildings about 150 yards away. (Note: If there are growing crops in this field, it might be better to follow the hedge round the field to the farm buildings.)

Carry on past the building along a track for 200 yards to where the track turns sharp right at some other buildings. Here go straight ahead and in about 200 yards, Campden School playing fields are reached. Carry straight on along the track (do NOT take a signposted track to the right just past the playing fields), until the road is reached.

Turn right at the road and first left, keeping the church on the left: past the almshouses until the main Campden street is reached. Here turn left and walk for about 500 yards. At the Catholic Church, turn right and in 150 yards, where the road turns right, carry straight on up a road – then track – signposted to Dovers Hill (and Cotswold Way).

Carry straight on up the hill for ½ mile to the road: turn left and in about 150 yards take a signposted footpath on the right. In 300 yards, go over a stile on to Dovers Hill. Turn left and in 450 yards, the National Trust car park where the walk started is reached.

RAMBLE 8

BLOCKLEY, DRAYCOTT, NORTHWICK PARK, DOVEDALE

Map 151 in the 1:50000 series.
Starting point Grid ref. 165350 – Blockley Parish Church.
Distance 5½ miles

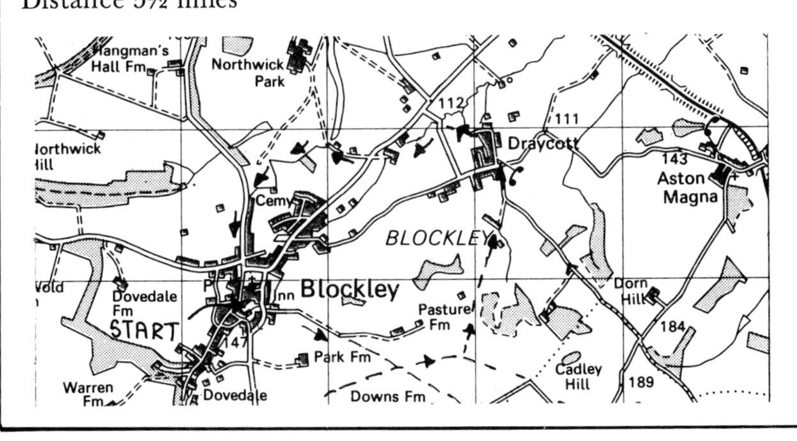

Start at the church gate by the Royal British Legion Club.

Enter the churchyard and take the left hand path: go down the path with the church on the right, to the road. Turn right to go past Lower Brook Hotel. Take the first turn on the left, sign-posted to Pasture Farm, by the brook. Follow the road to a point where it swings left with Pasture Farm buildings about 250 yards ahead. Here leave the farm road and go ahead up the field keeping close to the hedge on the right. Pass through a wicket gate and continue upwards towards a line of trees, passing through a second wicket gate on the way up.

At the top of the ascent, bear left with a stone wall on the right and continue over a stile to a wicket gate. Pass through and in about 30 yards, go through a gate on the left. Standing with your back to the gate, go half right (compass bearing 30°) across a field for about 250 yards to a point where two wire fences meet (marker post): go down rough stone steps in the bank into the next field with a wire fence on the left. Continue downhill, with a treed valley some 150 yards on the right for about 500 yards to a small facing copse: follow the headland round and with a hedge on the left, continue the descent to a facing hedge, the boundary of a garden: turn right and in 20 yards go through a wicket gate (there is also a stile for the more energetic walker), along a grass track with a stream on the right to a farm road. Follow this farm road till it joins the highway and continue ahead to Draycott.

Go over the cross roads and walk down the main street. Turn left at the end of the street in front of a facing farm house and in 70 yards, at a fork, continue ahead to a gate. Veer right (compass bearing 300°) crossing the field to arrive at a point where a stream (Blockley Brook) passes under the road. Go over a stile to the road and turn left. In about 120 yards enter, through a gap in the hedge, the field on the right. Cross this field (bearing 260°) to a fence in facing hedge about 25 yards from Blockley Brook. Enter next field: veer slight left to arrive at a rough stile in hedge and a small wooden bridge over a little stream: cross into next field. Continue ahead with hedge on the right to a stile near the corner of the field and with an old mill and buildings on the right. (Note: the mill has been converted into cottages). Pass in front of the cottages to the road.

Cross the road and walk down the metalled drive opposite. Just before the drive enters the grounds of Northwick Park, go through a gate on the left. Follow the stone wall on the right and enter a coppice. On emerging from this, and still keeping the stone wall on the right, ascend the hill to a gate on the right which gives access by a green track to Northwick Park. At this gate, turn left and go up the rise in front passing some large trees. At the top of this rise, go through a metal gate seen about 100 yards ahead to the metalled road: turn left and enter Blockley.

BOURTON DOWNS & HINCHWICK VALLEY

A beautiful valley, pleasant downs, some woodland and a charming hamlet.

Map 151 on the 1:50000 scale.
Grid ref. 154324 – near Bourton Hill House.
Distance 5 miles.

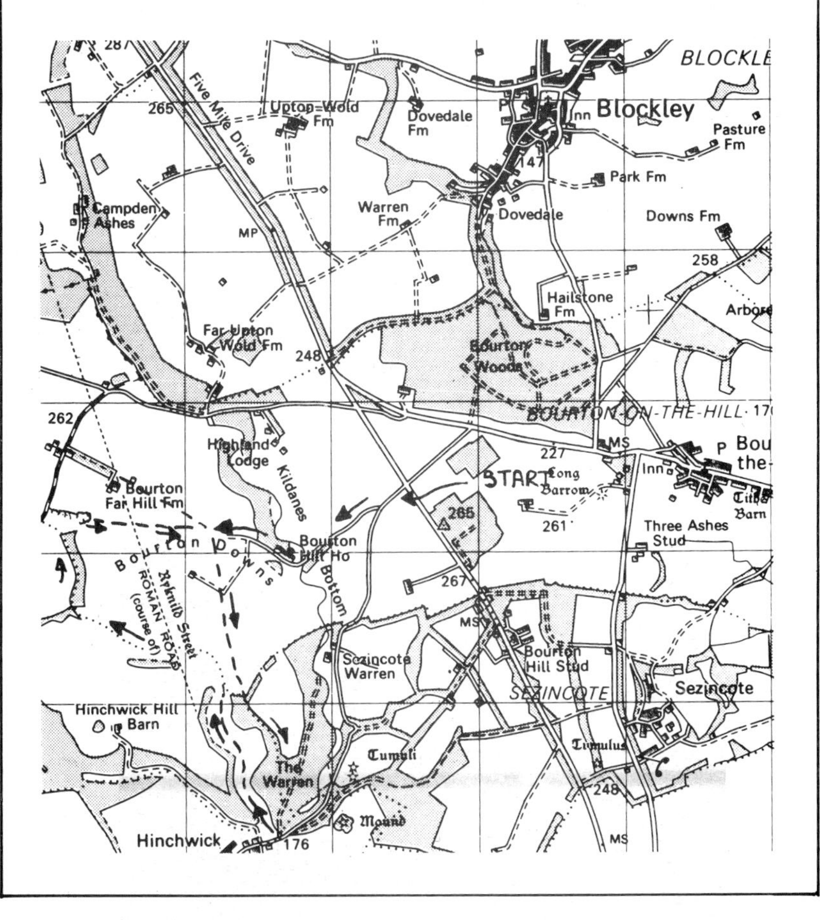

To get to the starting point from Broadway, go up Fish Hill. In about 6 miles, leave the A44 and take the A424, the Stow Road. Go over the next cross road and then take the next turn to the right. This is the start of the walk.

In 100 yards, there is a farm road on the right leading to Bourton Hill House. Go down this road and pass Bourton Hill House which is on the right. Ascend the road, passing to the left of some cottages. Near the top of the ascent, and after the first gate, there is a break on the left. Go along this with the conifer hedge on your left at first, *followed by a wire fence, to the corner of the field. Turn right and in 50 yards go down a track on the left, keeping the field wall on your right. In about 300 yards, pass through a gate and turn sharply left. Keep the fence on your left until you reach a gate on your left.* (The description in italics is not the right of way, but it is the one the landowner and farmer prefer to be followed). At this point, veer away from the fence towards the wood ahead.

Go into the wood through a bridle gate and follow the path, avoiding any side paths leading down into the valley on the right. The path leads to a T-junction with a well defined hard track. Turn right along this and descend to the road. At the road, turn right into Hinchwick. At the cross roads turn right through a gate, which is opposite to the road signposted Condicote. In about 20 yards go across the field on the right towards the right hand side of the wood directly ahead and towards a gate with a sheepfold on the left of it.

Proceed along the bottom of the valley between two woods and passing through three gates in fences, keeping the hedge or fence on your right until you come to a point where the boundaries of four fields meet. Go through the bridle gate and, in the next field, immediately turn right through a gate and continue in the same direction but with the fence or broken wall now on your left. Pass over a stile or through a fence into a wood and go ahead with the wall still on your left and a steep slope on your right for about 500 yards. The track turns slightly uphill for a few yards then, at a crossing with another path, there is a bridle gate on the left leading into an adjacent field. Do NOT go through the gate, but ascend the path on the right through the wood into an open field.

Follow the hedge and fence of this field, which is on the left until it becomes a definite track which eventually leads to Bourton Hill House. Continue ahead and so rise up to the road and the beginning and end of the walk.

RAMBLE 10

WINCHCOMBE – PRESCOTT

Map OS 163 in the 1:50000 series.
Distance 8½ miles.
Starting point: grid reference 025285 – Winchcombe car park adjacent to Public Library.

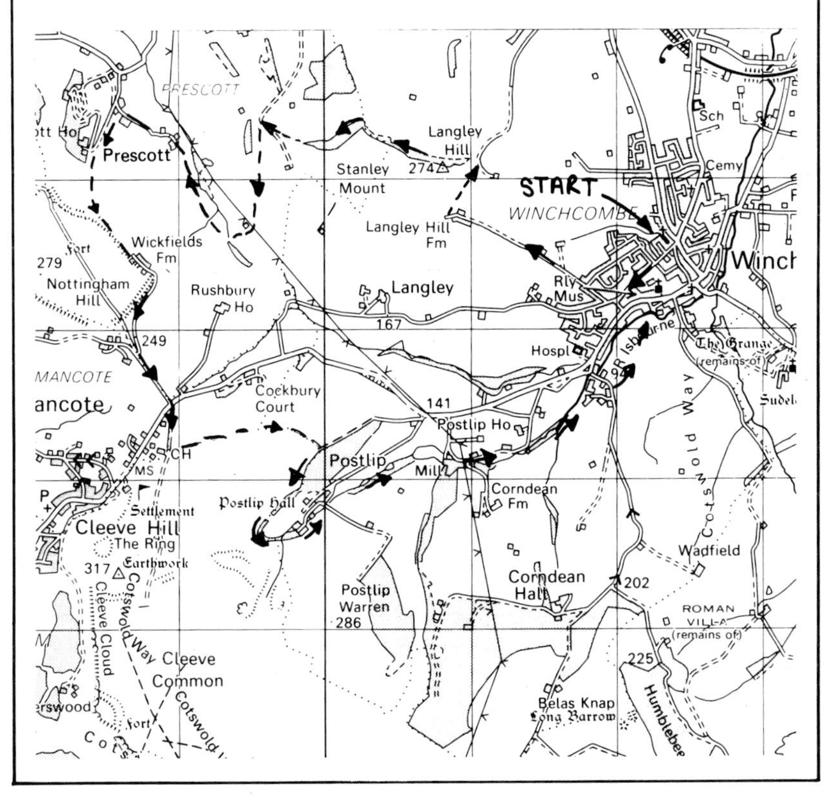

From the car park, turn left along road, bearing right at road junction and in a few yards, turn right up Harveys Road (sign-posted) and continue straight ahead uphill passing through Langley Hill Farm. 100 yards past the farm buildings, go through gate on right and almost immediately turn right along track across field to a gate 150 yards in front. Go through and bear right along track, which gradually becomes sunken, for about 300 yards to a W way sign (W is the Wychavon Way waymark): here turn left and follow wall on the right (ignore tracks on the left which lead to the summit of Langley Hill).

Where the track forks, take the definite track to the left (NOT the one to the right leading to a gate into a field) and follow the track, with W way signs, below the wooded slopes on the left. Pass through a gate and continue along the track following the W signs until rough farm ruins are reached; (here the W sign indicates going straight on – do NOT follow this), still continue on the distinct track and in 60 yards pass through a gate. Go on ahead with wooded slopes still on left for ¼ mile on rough ground to go through a bridle gate: continue for a further 500 yards to the end of the wood. Carry on in the same direction to a stone wall: bear right downhill with wire fence and line of small trees on the left. At the bottom of the field, go through a gate on the left; walk ahead for 60 yards to another gate to a track with trees on both sides and fence on left. In about 200 yards pass through the right hand of two gates and carry on downhill with wire fence on right to a gate; pass through, turn left and go through another gate 30 yards on left into a field, which cross, keeping hedge on left.

Pass into another field at the beginning of which is a small barn under some power lines. Immediately turn right to descend with fence on right. Go through bridle gate at the bottom of field: walk ahead for about 30 yards and turn right in the field keeping hedge on the left about 60 yards away to arrive at facing hedge. Pass into the next field through a bridle gate with hedge immediately on left. Veer away right and downhill from this hedge for 150 yards to facing hedge and cross small stream over a bridge into next field. Proceed in same direction with stream on right to Manor Farm Prescott, keeping house and farm buildings on left, to a wicket gate leading on to the metalled road.

Carry on along the road passing a few houses until just after The Mill House. Turn sharp left and ascend the bridleway for about 300 yards to the junction of a track coming in from the right. Here bear left and in 30 yards carry on in the same direction ascending the bridleway with a ruined house on the left. (Note: by turning right at this point and walking for a few yards, Prescott House may be seen.)

Walk on uphill till Wickfields Farm (marked on some maps as Prescott Hill Farm) is reached, beyond which take the metalled road which swings right to a subsidiary road; turn left and continue ahead to main road A46.

Cross the A46 and go ahead up the road towards Golf Club. Pass through gate into Cleeve Common and immediately turn left and follow the track gradually downhill to a junction of tracks passing through two gates. At this cross junction, take the descending one ahead. In 200 yards, at another cross junction, bear right and carry on to the bottom of the valley, keeping the wood on the left. At a Cotswold Way marker post turn left over a waymarked stile into a copse and thence to an open field which cross keeping wire fence on left to a gate in facing fence; go through; turn right and go over stile ahead, turn half left to gate into track. Here turn right, through some farm buildings, cross road and through facing wicket gate, keeping high stone wall on left. (Note: If the grass bank on the right is climbed a little way, a good view of Postlip Hall and the tythe barn is obtained.)

Cross the road to a public footpath between wire fences (marked "Public Footpath to Winchcombe") and parallel to stream. Follow this clearly defined path for about 400 yards, over a number of stiles keeping the stream and thick rough area on the left until, at a point about 15 yards from the end of a field a concrete slab forming a bridge over the stream will be seen. Cross this and turn right to the paper mill in front. At the car park, follow the road round to the left, and leaving the mill fire station on the right, ascend the road to a T junction. Here turn right to enter the mill premises again (this is somewhat circuitous, but it seems to follow the right of way through the mill property).

Continue straight ahead for about 300 yards to pass through an iron kissing gate. In a further 150 yards, the road bears left. Here go straight ahead over a stile into a field and in the same direction cross the field, over another stile and over two more fields to the road on the outskirts of Winchcombe. In 20 yards turn right up Corndean Lane for about 170 yards. Go left over the righthand of two stiles. Cross two fields keeping the hedge on the left (a view of Sudeley Castle half right is obtained here): over a stile into an open field: turn left: go through facing hedge into a small field. Descend the bank to a bridge over stream (R. Isbourne) to a gate and stile and then into Mill Lane and the main street of Winchcombe. Turn right, pass the church and then take the first small lane to the left. In about 150 yards the car park and the start of the walk is reached.

RAMBLE 11

SEVEN SPRINGS, CHARLTON KINGS COMMON, HARTLEY COTTAGES

A walk mostly at high level, with fine views over Cheltenham.
Map OS 163 in the 1:50000 series.
Starting point grid reference 969171 – Seven Springs.
Distance 4½ miles.

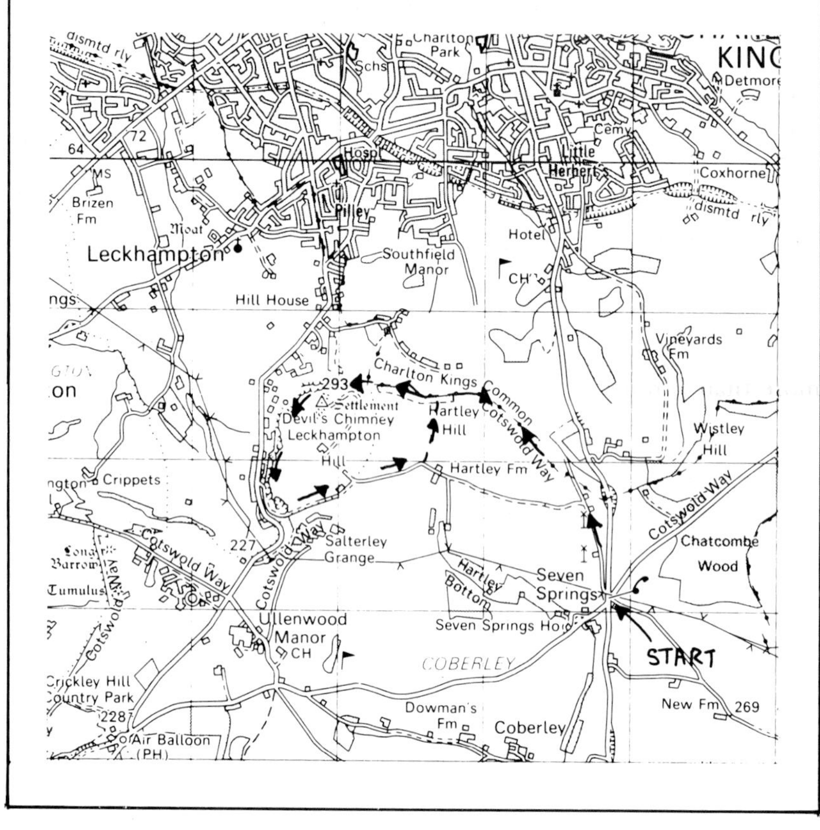

To get to Seven Springs, leave Cheltenham on the A435 and in 1¾ miles, a main crossing is reached which is the start of the ramble.

Park on the space at the right hand side of the cross roads. **Take great care at these dangerous cross roads.**

The walk begins here.

Go back on the A435 towards Cheltenham and in 60 yards go up the minor road on the left. In less than ½ mile, the road turns sharply left; here leave the road and take the definite track ahead. In about 200 yards, leave the definite track by turning left at a Cotswold Way sign. Ascend a field with a hedge on the left. In about 75 yards, turn right at another Cotswold Way sign and follow the hedge which is on the left and continue ahead through a copse. Now follow the Cotswold Way signs keeping to the top of the ridge and avoiding any paths which descend to the right.

In about 1½ miles from leaving that minor road, the way emerges on to an open field. Follow the right hand boundary of this field for about 150 yards and then take a path on the right which leads to a signpost indicating the Devil's Chimney. This is a fantastic piece of stone which was left during quarrying operations in about 1780.

After seeing it, return to the signpost and continue ahead for over ½ mile, along the definite track with views of the valley on the right, and descend to the road.

Turn left. Go along the road for about ¾ mile to Hartley Farm. Immediately past the last building on the left, turn left off the road into the field. Follow the wall which is on the left for more than ½ mile.

Pass over a stile on to Charlton Kings Common. Turn right and now follow in the reverse direction the way taken at the beginning of the walk back to Seven Springs.

RAMBLE 12

ULLENWOOD, CRICKLEY HILL COUNTRY PARK, AIR BALLOON INN, THE PEAK

A high level walk with splendid views.
Map OS 163 in the 1:50000 series.
Starting point grid reference 931152 a minor road off the A417 just ½ mile north of Birdlip.
Distance 6½ miles.

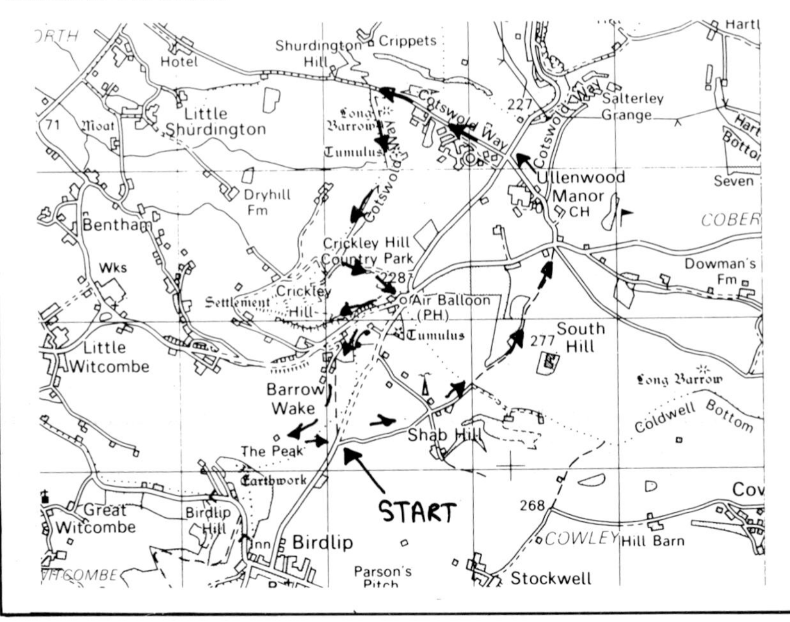

From Birdlip – Go north for ½ mile and start the walk from the first road on the right.

From Cheltenham – Go out south on the B4070 and in 4 miles pass over the cross roads at the Air Balloon Inn and continue south on the A417(T). Start the walk at the second turn on the left.

Go along this road and in less than ½ mile, continue ahead over the cross roads. Notice the masts of Winstone Radio Station on the left. In a further 400 yards, the road terminates, but proceed in the same direction along the definite track for ¾ mile to the road (A436). Cross the road and go up the road opposite. This is now part of the Cotswold Way. Follow this road for ½ mile to the cross roads. Cross the road B4070 and go up the road opposite.

Go ahead for about ¾ mile. Immediately beyond a copse, the road forks. Go left and in a few yards take a footpath on the left up some steps signposted Crickley Hill.

Follow the Cotswold Way signs, with fine views of the valley on the right, for nearly 1½ miles through woodland. Where the track comes out of the wood veer right to a wicket gate. Pass into the road, which is now part of the Crickley Hill Country Park. Cross the road into the wood opposite indicated by the National Trust notice. Follow the track to the road (A436) near the Air Balloon Inn. Refreshments may be had here.

At the road A436, descend to the right. In about 500 yards cross the road and go down the service road on the left. Follow it round to the right. In a few yards go through a kissing gate on the left with a Cotswold Way sign. Ascend for a time and then continue ahead as the way levels out.

The way continues alongside the steep slope on the left. Keep to the bottom of this slope and go through a gate following Cotswold Way signs.

Continue ahead until Hill Farm is seen a few yards to the right. Now ascend the bank on the left, which is very steep, to the top: this is The Peak. Turn right; go over a stile into a wood and in about 150 yards, go through the first gate on the left into a field. Proceed ahead following the wire fence on the left and an open field on the right. Pass over a stile into some common land and follow a path to two toposcopes near the main road A417(T). Turn right for about 50 yards to the beginning of the walk.

WITHINGTON, WITHINGTON WOODS, CASSEY COMPTON, RIVER COLN

Distance 8 miles.
Map OS 163 in the 1:50000 series.
Starting point grid reference 033154 – Village of Withington
Withington is 8 miles SE of Cheltenham.

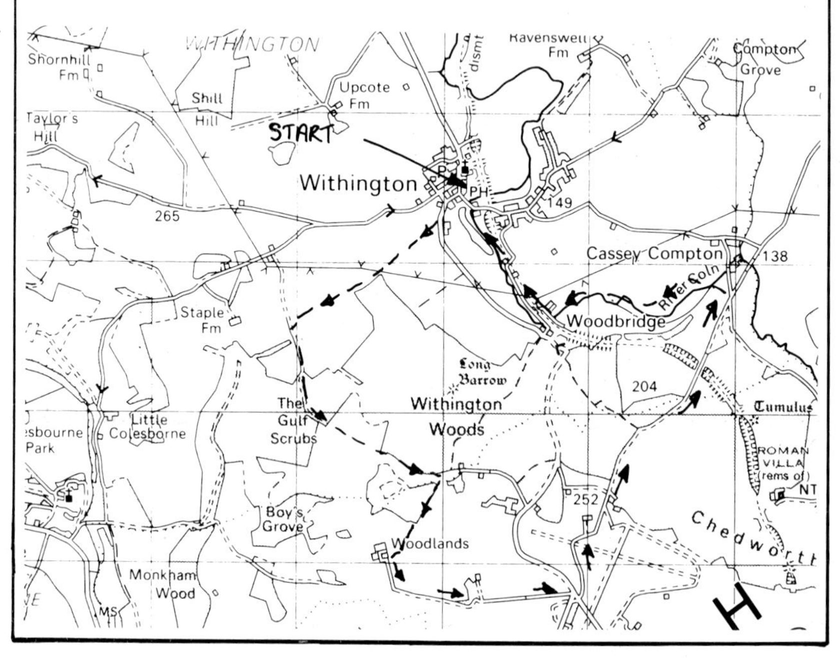

From the Mill Inn go along the road over the River Coln and up the hill. Take the first turn on the left and in 100 yards, turn left again. In about 150 yards from this turning, pass over a fence on the right in the corner of the field. From here, veer left SW (compass bearing 220°) ascending the field to arrive at a facing fence. (If barbed wire is a problem, there is a gate some yards to the right). Now go at right angles to this fence towards a space between a wood on the left and a line of trees on the right (compass bearing 248° from the facing fence and NOT from the diversion through the gate). Pass under some electricity lines preceding this space to arrive at a gate. If in doubt, this gate is about 200 yards from the field boundary on the right. (That describes the right of way, but a simple way and one which the farmer would probably prefer would be as follows: After going from the road over the fence in the corner of the field, follow the fence on the right to a gate. Pass into the next field and continue ahead with the hedge on the right to a facing hedge. Here turn left and walk with the hedge on the right for approximately 200 yards. Pass under some power lines and turn right up a gulley to a gate in a fence.)

Pass into the next field. Follow the fence which is on the left to a large upright stone (remains of an old stile) in the corner of the field. Turn right and in 60 yards, go through a gate on the left.

Turn right so that the fence is now on the right and, at the corner of the field, turn left. Follow the fence which is on the right, for about 500 yards until it meets a farm track.

Turn left and follow the track, or lane, which rises slightly, towards a wood. At the top of the rise the track comes to a gate which opens into a field. Cross the field keeping parallel to, and 30 or 40 yards from the hedge on the right to a gate in the hedge ahead. A telecommunications tower should be visible on the skyline in this direction. This leads into an area of scrub with large rearing cages for pheasants on the right of the path. (These cages may be temporary.) At the end of the cages the ground falls slightly and on the right an open field can be seen through a gap in the trees. A cross track is clear to the left but rather indistinct to the right. Take the path to the right which leads to a stile in the gap which pass over into the field.

Continue ahead with the wood on the right to the corner of the wood. Keep ahead in the same direction making slightly to the left of the farm buildings of Woodlands Farm. A small bridge crosses a stream or ditch and leads on to a hard road. Bear right through the farm yard following the waymarks. In about 300 yards there are some bridleway and footpath signposts; ignore these and bear left by following the definite track. In ¾ mile, the main road is reached. The signposts read Withington and Andoversford to the left and Chedworth 1 mile ahead. Cross this road and in 20 yards, another sign reads Compton Abdale (gated road). Turn left along this road.

In about 1 mile, the road passes over a disused railway by a bridge. The road rises slightly from here for about 100 yards and then descends towards Cassey Compton, but in 150 to 200 yards from the top of the rise, there is a fence on the left with a stile and a waymark. Go over this into the field and follow the sunken grass track. Bear left about half way down the descent to go round the hill above Cassey Compton. Having gone round the hill, drop down to a fence and pass through the gate in the corner of the field. Keep the wire fence on the right and cross the stream by the footbridge which is waymarked. There is a stile before the bridge.

Follow the fence which is on the left and pass over a stile. Ascend with a fence on the right and pass through a facing gate. Turn left and go ahead with a hedge and fence on the left to a stile. Go over the stile and continue in the same direction on the side of the hill. On coming to a hedge going in the same direction, keep to the right of it for ¼ mile passing over a stone wall by a stile in the course of the ¼ mile. Pass to the right of a cottage, turn half right to a gate with a Cotswold Way sign.

Pass through on to a definite track and go through the old railway bridge. In a few yards at a T junction, turn right. Go ahead along the definite track for 400 yards. Where the road turns sharply right between the walls of the railway embankment, and by a derelict building on the left, leave the road by turning left behind the building and follow the signposted path by the River Coln. Go through the back of the Old Mill buildings and so on to the road in Withington.

KILKENNY, UPPER HILCOT, FOXCOTE, SHILL HILL

A fine walk with wonderful views from the ridges.
Map OS 163 in the 1:50000 series.
Starting point grid reference 004186 – near the Kilkenny Inn.
Distance – 1st part 4 miles; 2nd part 4½ miles.
This can be considered as two separate walks from Kilkenny.

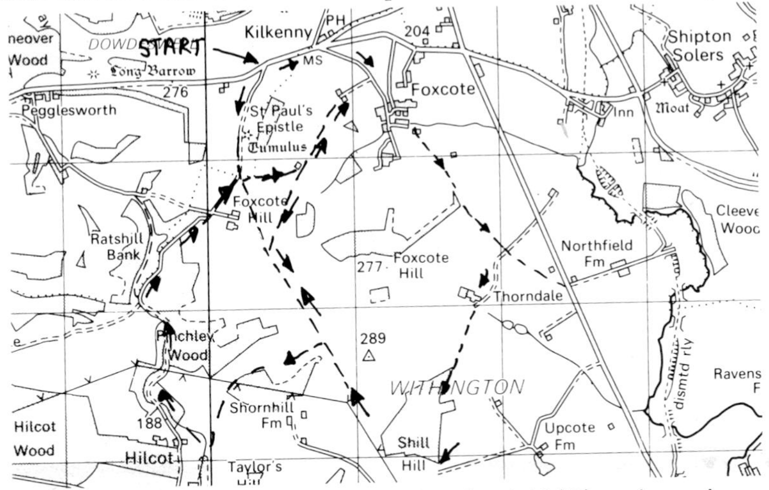

If travelling from Cheltenham, leave by the A40(T) and continue on it until the fork with the A435 is reached. This is to the right. Follow it and in roughly 3 miles at the cross roads known as Seven Springs (grid ref. 969171) turn left. In a little over 3 miles turn right, signposted "Parking: Viewpoint".

The walk starts from the car park here.

On leaving the car park, turn left up the road, and in 500 yards, pass a treed mound (tumulus) known as "St Paul's Epistle". (A former parish priest with some parishioners was accustomed to walking the parish bounds and at this point would always read one of St Paul's Epistles.)

In a further 300 yards, where the open field on the left ends at a coppice, turn left along the headland with a stone wall on the right, and walk for 50 yards to a stile on the right. Go over and cross two more stiles on the right of an enclosed mound (water?) and continue ahead with a wall on the right and a wire fence on the left. Proceed to the end of the field, cross over the stile and keep the same direction to a gateway on the right.

Go through the gateway and immediately turn left and walk over two fields with a wall on the left. At the end of the second field, pass through a gate on the left, immediately turn right and follow a distinct track for 200 yards to where it forks near a strip of wood.

Go through a gate to the right and immediately pass through another gate on the right thus making a U turn.

Turn left and follow the wood on the left with an open field on the right and pass under some power lines. In a further 20 yards, go through a gate on the left into a coppice and immediately turn right.

Keep to the ridge following a track through the shrubs. After about 50 yards, drop slightly to a clearing on the left and carry on along this ridge for 150 yards or so. At this point where the shrubs have thinned out, descend to a path. Follow it as it descends diagonally towards the black and white farm seen below. This is Upper Hilcot (admire the view as you descend). Continue to the valley floor, pass over a brook, with a pond on the right, and ascend to Upper Hilcot.

Turn right at the road. In roughly ¾ mile, ignore the track on the left and keep straight ahead. After a further ½ mile, pass over a farm cross road and go on along the road to the car park.

4 miles have now been walked.

Turn right on leaving the car park and right again at the main road to reach the Kilkenny Inn in 500 yards. Refreshments may be had here.

Now follows the second part of the walk.

Cross the road from the Inn (very busy road) to the little lane opposite, signposted Foxcote. Drop to the hamlet bearing right as the entrance drive to Foxcote Manor is passed: a disused Baptist chapel will be seen on the right.

At the end of the road, go right towards the entrance of a private house before which a stile on the right will take you into a field.

Follow the hedge on the left for 40 yards. Where the hedge

goes to the left, continue up the field, but veer left to a hedge almost at the top of the rise. Follow this to the left to a gate. Go through, veer right (SE bearing 140°) to reach another gate near a strip of wood. This leads to a definite track which follow to the right to a road.

Turn along the road and pass along the left of Thorndale Farm. Go through the farm gate ahead into a field. From here, walk diagonally across the field (SSW bearing 200°) and make for the left hand edge of a wood seen ahead.

Go through the gate into the wood and walk along the definite track at the edge of the wood for ½ mile with views over the wall on the left.

On leaving the wood, turn right to follow a track at the edge of a field. Ascend the field with trees on the left to reach a gateway. Go through and immediately turn right along a hedge. In 250 yards, pass a waterhole which is on the left in some rough ground. (The waterhole may be so overgrown that it may be difficult to see). Veer left to a gate in the facing hedge.

Go through and ascend the field, keeping alongside the wall on the right. Pass into the next field, at the end of which pass through a gate and continue ahead with a wall on the left. In 300 yards go through a gate on the left and keep in the same direction, the wall now being on the right. Walk over two fields and, at the end of the second one go through the gate on the right.

Now take the descending track ahead (NNE bearing 22°) which drops to the ruins of a farm building. Pass through a gate and follow the definite track back to the minor road. Turn left and in 400 yards the Kilkenny Inn is reached.

RAMBLE 15

LINEOVER WOOD, KILKENNY, UPPER HILCOT, PEGGLEWORTH

An interesting walk with fine ridge views.
Map OS 163 in the 1:50000 series.
Distance 7½ miles.
Starting point grid reference 984183 on the A436.

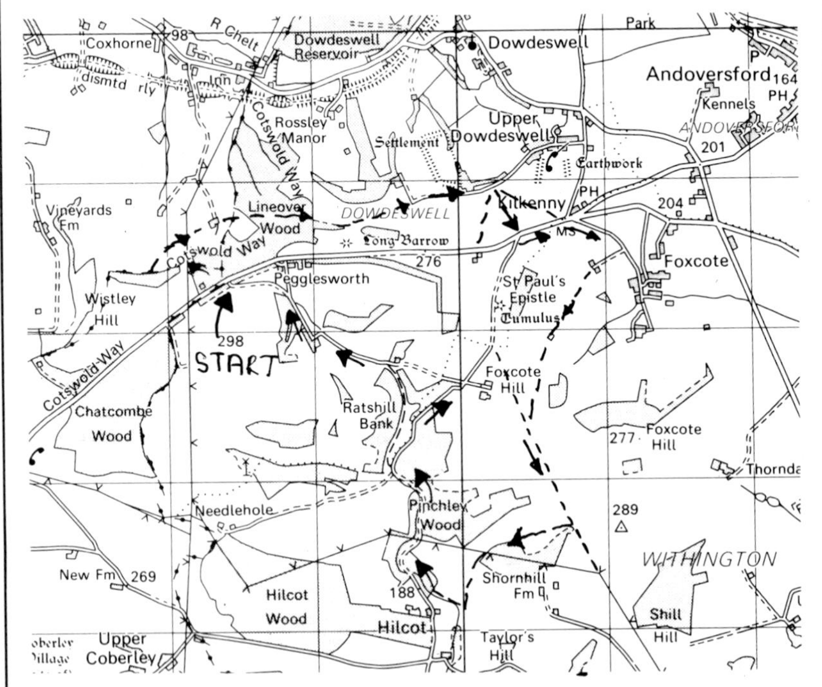

To get to the starting point, leave Cheltenham going south on the A435. In about 1½ miles at Seven Springs turn left to A436. In about 1¼ miles on the right there is the first entrance to Peggleworth Home Farm with a notice requesting that the footpath should be kept to as it is a private road. Opposite on the other side of the road is a wide footpath. This is the start of the walk.

Go down this footpath with a wall on the right and a fence on the left. At the point where the wire fence goes sharp left, continue ahead bearing left and descending in a wood. Follow the definite path to leave the wood at a bridle gate. Turn slightly left and go to the left of an electricity pylon. In about 60 yards, follow the fence alongside a wood which is on the left. There are now splendid views to the right.

In a further 300 yards, there is a gate on the left with a Cotswold Way sign (an arrow with a white dot). Do not go through this gate but turn right for a few yards to another Cotswold Way sign on a post. From here follow the steep descending path on the side of the hill to the valley below.

Continue along the path to a bridle gate with another Cotswold Way sign. Go through the gate and some trees into a field. Continue ahead downhill, keeping well to the right of the farmhouse seen below, to a gate with a Cotswold Way sign on a post. Carry on to a gate with another Cotswold Way sign to enter Lineover Wood.

In about 300 yards, after entering the wood the path forks: go to the right. Leave the wood through a gate with a Cotswold Way sign. DO NOT FOLLOW THIS SIGN, but go ahead so as to have the wood on the right 20 yards away. Ascend to and pass through a gate. Here turn left along a definite track. This leads to a gate alongside a barn. Pass through the gate and continue ahead along the metalled track.

In 600 yards at the top of an ascent, there are 2 gates on the right: go through the left hand one. Go over 2 fields following a hedge which is on the right. At the road A436, turn left to the Kilkenny Inn.

Go down the road which is opposite the Inn signposted Foxcote. In about 400 yards, go through a gate on the right which is opposite a gate on the other side of the road, and proceed along the definite farm track. Pass through a gate and go through an open field following a fence which is on the left. Ascend to the ridge.

Pass through the gate ahead in the facing wall running along the top of the ridge. Immediately turn left and follow the wall, not on the left, over two fields to a gate on the left. Go through and turn right and follow the distinct open track for 200 yards to where the track forks near a strip of wood. Go through the gate to the right. Turn right and immediately go through another gate on the right: so that a U-turn has been made. Turn left and follow the wood which is on the left, with an open field to the right, and pass under some electricity power lines.

In a further 20 yards go through a gate on the left and follow the track (often overgrown) to the right keeping to the ridge. In a few yards, descend slightly to the clearing on the left. Follow this to the right along the ridge for about 150 yards.

At this point, where the shrubs have thinned out, descend to a path. Follow this path as it descends diagonally towards the black and white farm seen below at Upper Hilcot. Admire the view as you go down. Continue to the bottom of the valley, pass over a brook with a pond on the right, and ascend to Upper Hilcot.

At the road, turn right. In about ¾ mile, a track comes in from the left, but continue ahead and in a further ½ mile, there is a farm cross roads. Turn left to Peggleworth Home Farm. Pass through the farm and continue along the road.

Where the road forks, do not go to the right to the hamlet of Peggleworth, but continue along the road to the left to the A436 and the end and beginning of the walk.

UPPER COBERLEY, COCKLEFORD, COWLEY

An interesting ramble with some remote exploration
Map OS 163 in the 1:50000 series
Distance 11 miles

Starting point grid reference 978158, the hamlet of Upper Coberley
A shorter ramble of 5½ miles may be made by starting from Cockleford (map reference 969142). How to do this is shown by the note at the end of the longer walk.

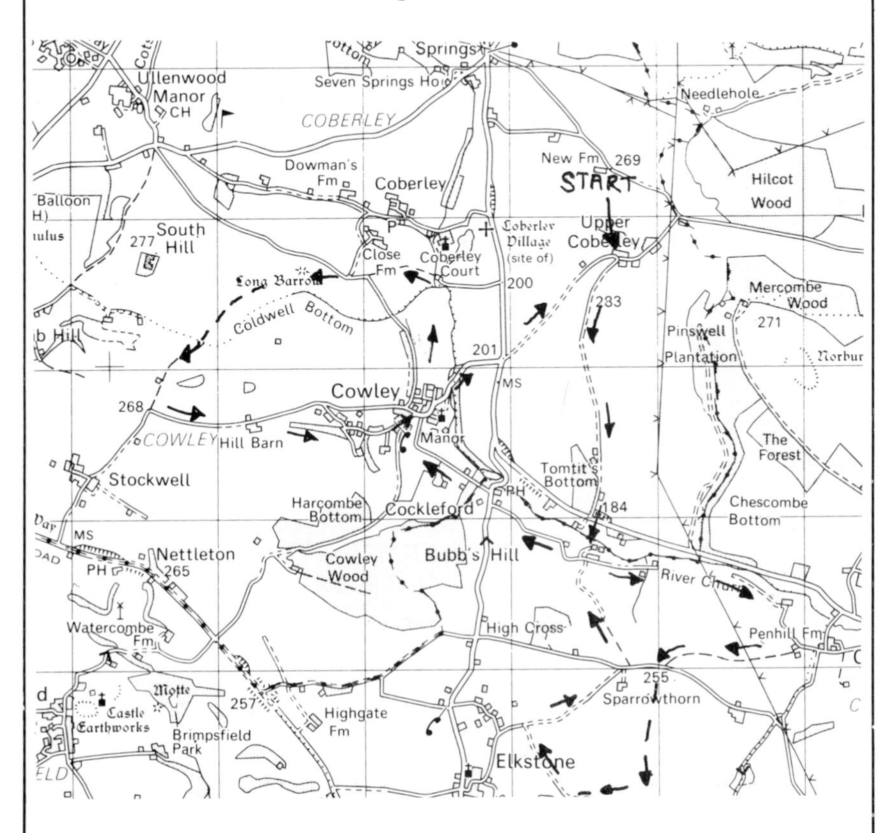

To get to Upper Coberley from Cheltenham, go out on A40(T) and, before leaving the town, fork right at the traffic lights, taking the A435. In about 4½ miles, leave the A435 and, opposite the road signposted Cowley, take the road left. This is the road to Upper Coberley, and is not signposted. The ramble begins at the hamlet where car parking is very restricted.

At the top of the hill at the beginning of the hamlet, facing the gateway to Lower Farm, there is a bridleway on the right. Walk along the bridleway without deviation. Continue to the left of a large barn. The bridleway now becomes a metalled road. Just before the main road, there is a wood on the right called Tomtits Bottom.

Cross the main road A435, and go down the track opposite to pass in front of Cockleford Mill – a house in a charming setting – to a footbridge. Cross over the river Churn; go up the path and, at the subsidiary road, turn left. In about ¼ mile, just before a house called Churn Bank, pass through a gate on to a bridleway.

(The description of the shorter walk from Cockleford comes in at this point. See note at the end.)

Follow the bridleway across the field with a hedge on the left and, in about 300 yards, bear left, still on the bridleway, through a gate into a small field. Carry on in same direction, pass a farm and continue to the road.

Follow the road to the right. In about 350 yards, there are 2 houses on the right where the road turns left. Go up the definite track on the right through a field gate between these 2 houses. Follow the enclosed track for about 500 yards. Go through a gate into a field. It is now open on the left and there is a hedge on the right. Follow this hedge for a few yards and pass again into an enclosed track. Go through a bridle gate and continue ahead to an open field. Follow the fence on the right to where it turns right downhill and here leave the fence and carry on ahead veering left along an indefinite, but evident track to a gate giving access to the road. Turn right.

In about 300 yards, go through the first gate on the left which precedes Sparrowthorn Farm.

Keeping a hedge and small stream on the left, go over a double gate. Continue ahead down the field for some 500 yards till a facing hedge is reached at the bottom of the descent. Turn right and walk along a track with a fence and stream on the left for about 600 yards to where the track forks. Take the right hand ascending track with a small wood on the left and carry on; take the right hand gate and continue up the track over 3 fields with first a wall and then a fence on the left. At the top of the rise a definite track fenced on both sides will lead to a cross track; turn right on this clearer track and follow it to the minor road.

(Halfway up the ascending track, the village of Elkstone can be seen on the left with a track leading to it. The church is most interesting and well worth a diversion. It is unusual in having a columbarium (dove-cote) over the chancel, reached by a newel stairway near the pulpit.)

At the minor road, turn right and in about 60 yards go through a gate on the left; descend from the gate veering left along a faint track towards a small wood seen ahead. Pass to the left of this wood. Descend to and go through a gate. Continue descending veering half left to a distinct grass track which leads down to the road. Turn left and at the T junction, turn right to the Green Dragon Inn at Cockleford.

(The shorter walk starts and ends here.)

Go along the road directly opposite the Green Dragon, and in a little while Cowley Manor will be seen on the right. At the T junction turn right. Follow the road round past the gates of the Manor. Where the road bends to the right, take the track on the left (with a notice "Churnside Camp and Adventure Centre").

Go along with a hedge and wall on the left. At the end of the wall carry on in the same direction over a stile in a fence. Go over the field passing to the right of a small coppice to a gap in the boundary hedge. Go through this gap and immediately turn left and walk with the hedge on the left to the corner of the field. Follow the track round to the right with the hedge on the left.

In about 80 yards, go through the hedge on the left and follow a path to a footbridge. From the bridge, ascend the other bank, veer to the right and follow a wire fence to a gate and a stile (there is a footpath sign on the other side of the lane – ignore this). Pass over the stile and immediately turn left along a green lane for some 300 yards, pass into the next field, still on the green lane, keeping the hedge on the right until the road is reached.

Go along this road for about 150 yards and just past the road junction, go through a gate on the left into a field and walk along a banked green track with a wall on the right for about 200 yards. When the track forks, go to the left. Continue ahead through a gate. Proceed in the same direction and descend to another gate which go through. (There is another path to the right of this gate, which ignore.) Follow the green track with a wall on the right and a wire fence on the left; through a gate and, in about 150 yards at the bottom of a hill in front, turn left and ascend by some trees to a gate with a barn on the right. Go through the gate and ascend in the same direction with a wood and stream on the right, to a gate. Go through and turn left to the road.

Turn left and in about ¼ mile, immediately past Hill Barn Farm, go through a gate on the right and walk diagonally across the little field to a wicket gate. Go through and follow a fence and wall on the right for 150 yards to a gate. Go through the gate and turn right for 5 yards, and then take the track on the left through the wood. Follow the track, which after about 200 yards, drops left-handed to a fence. With this fence on the left, carry on for about 200 yards, crossing a track, until a wicket gate is reached. Go through this and through the farm gate a few yards ahead, and thence to the road.

Walk along the road into Cowley, past the school on the left to the T junction. Turn right and follow the road past the entrance to Cowley Manor. Continue on this road over a bridge till the main road A435 is reached.

Cross the road and go up the road opposite and carry on to Upper Coberley.

To do the shorter walk, proceed as follows:

From the Green Dragon Inn at Cockleford (map reference 969142), walk up the road with the Inn on the left for 100 yards. Turn left. In about ¾ mile, just past a house called Churn Bank, pass through a gateway into a bridleway. Now follow the narrative at the point indicated by the note almost at the beginning of this narrative.

RAMBLE 17

COLESBOURNE, UPPER COBERLEY, LOWER COCKLEFORD

An easy ramble with some good views.

Map OS163 in the 1:50000 series.
Starting point grid reference 999132, Colesbourne Village.
Distance 6½ miles.

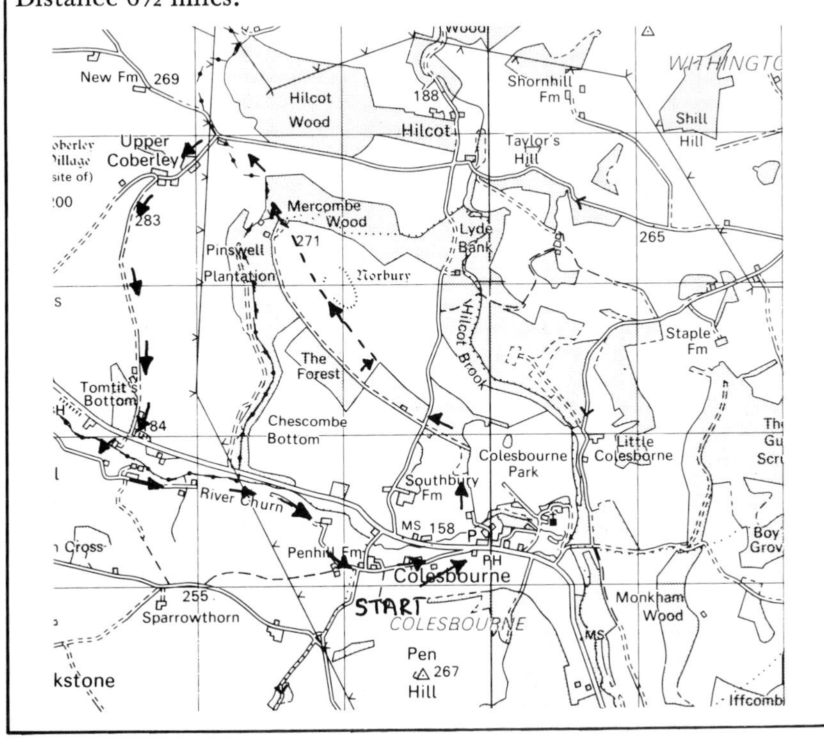

Go down the track to the right of, and adjacent to the parking area of the Colesbourne Inn.

Pass over the River Churn by a bridge and continue ahead. Where the cart track goes round to the left, leave it to ascend the field with a wood on the right. Go through a gate and immediately go through a kissing gate on the right into a field. Turn sharp left and ascend the field following the hedge, ditch and wall on the left.

In about 250 yards, there is a gate on the left. Go through into a treed definite cart track and follow this for 300 yards, and pass through a gateway with two stone pillars. Cross the road and continue up the rough road opposite.

Go ahead with a wood on the right. In just over ¼ mile, where the wood on the right ends, and another on the left begins, turn right up a cart track with the wood on the right and an open field on the left. In about 150 yards, follow the track round to the left. Go ahead for ¾ mile to join the rough road previously left, at a house on the left. Was this a toll house for the stage coach? Which was the high road?

Continue ahead for ¼ mile to the road. Turn left and, in less than 100 yards, turn left again and go into Upper Coberley. Leave the hamlet by the gateway of Lower Farm. Immediately through the gateway there is a bridleway on the left. Follow this without deviation to the main road A435.

Cross the road and go down the track opposite to pass in front of a charming house to a footbridge. Cross this bridge over the river Churn and go up the path. At the subsidiary road, turn left. In about ¼ mile, just before a house called Churn Bank, pass through a gate on to a bridleway. Follow this bridleway across the field with a hedge on the left and in about 300 yards, bear left still on the bridleway through a gate and continue with the hedge now on the right to another gateway. Go through and go ahead with the hedge now on the left for 200 yards and through a gate into a small field.

Carry on in the same direction, pass a farm and continue to the road. Follow the road to the right.

Go ahead for ¾ mile along the road back to Colesbourne.

RAMBLE 18

CAUDLE GREEN, BRIMPSFIELD PARK, CLIMPERWELL WOOD

A pleasant ramble by stream and woodland in an area not frequently visited by ramblers.
Map OS 163 in the 1:50000 series.
Starting point grid reference 943105 in the hamlet of Caudle Green.
Distance 5½ miles or 3¾ miles.

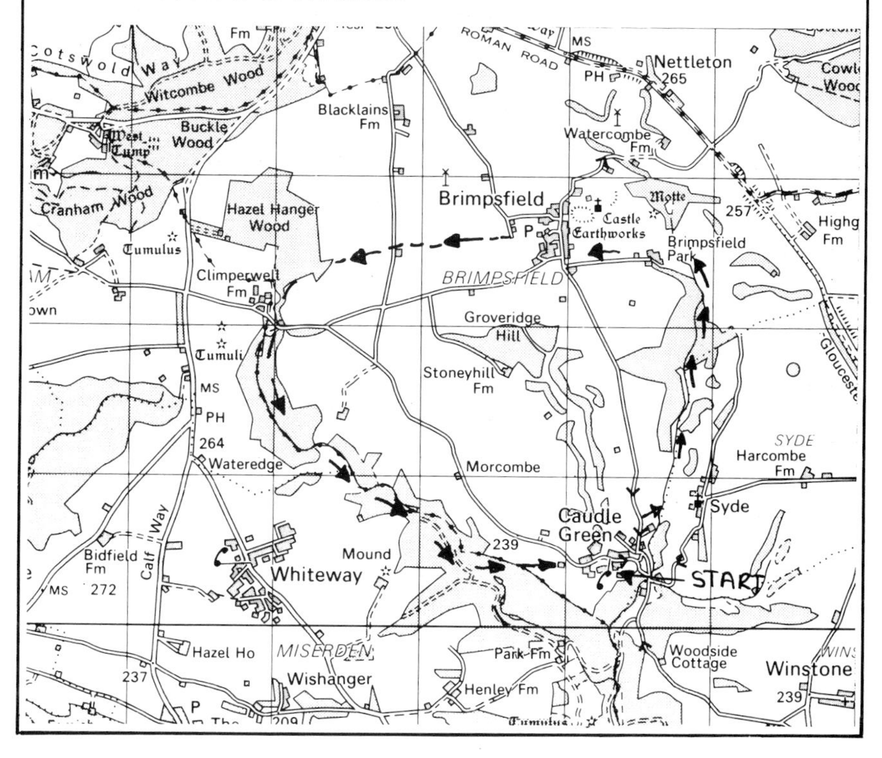

To get to Caudle Green from Cheltenham, go out on the A40(T) and before leaving the town, fork right at the traffic lights on to the A435. In about 5½ miles, take a road on the right signposted Elkstone. From Elkstone go west to A417(T), and turn left. In ¾ mile, take a road on the right and go through Syde to Caudle Green.

OR

Leave Cheltenham on A46. Before leaving the town, at a fork, go left along B4070 and continue to the Air Balloon Inn. From here go along A417(T) to Birdlip. In Birdlip turn left and in about 80 yards turn right and go through Brimpsfield to Caudle Green.

In Caudle Green, descend between the mail box and the telephone box. Thirty yards beyond the last cottage, where the road turns right, go over the stone stile in the wall. Go down the steep slope to a wall. Go through the gate, or over a stile in the wall, into the road. Ascend the road ahead with a house on your left. In 100 yards, turn right down the approach to a house.

Pass to the right of the house, go over a stile and between two giant Wellingtonias to a gate. After passing through the gate do NOT veer right towards Syde, but continue along the valley with a stream and fence on the left. Pass through a gate where an iron fence descends from the right. In a further 70 yards, cross the stream by stone slabs and continue ahead with the stream now on your right. Keep to the bottom of the valley for ¼ mile.

Enter a wood by a bridle gate where a wall comes down from the right. Immediately pass over the bridge to the other side of the stream. Go ahead up the valley through the wood, with the stream now on the left. On emerging from the wood, through a gate, continue ahead for about 40 yards, turn left, pass over the stream and through another gate and go along the farm track.

Follow the track to the buildings in Brimpsfield Park and then go along the farm road to another road forming a T junction. At this point a decision must be made whether to take the longer walk of 5½ miles, or the shorter one of 3¾ miles. The shorter walk will be described between the brackets.

(Turn left. In about 30 yards, go through a gate on the right. Follow a hedge which is on the right straight ahead for about 350 yards. Veer right to follow the track through a gate and descend to a conifer wood. Continue with this wood on the right for about 200 yards. Pass through a gate and follow on with woods on both sides. As this passage opens out, proceed ahead following the wood on the left down the valley. This leads to a track by the stream into Caudle Green. This brings you to the lower stone stile of the two at the beginning of the walk.)

Now continue with the longer walk:

At the T junction turn right towards Brimpsfield and in 50 yards turn left. In about 100 yards, at a house, fork right into a wide opening between the houses. In a further 40 yards, do not follow the road round to the right but go through the gate ahead into a field.

Walk with the hedge alongside on the right. At the end of this field, do not go through the facing gate, but turn left and follow alongside the hedge. Go over 3 fields and then enter a path between two hedges and continue to the road.

Cross the road into the field opposite through a gate. Follow the hedge which is on the right over 2 fields – having climbed a stile between the 2 fields – to enter a wood by a bridle gate. On leaving the wood, continue with a wood alongside on the right. In about 250 yards, take a path on the right as it leaves the field and descends with trees on each side. Go over a stile before reaching a junction with a definite farm track at which turn left.

On reaching the road near Climperwell, cross the road, at the entrance to Climperwell Cottage, and go down the cart track opposite into Climperwell Wood, passing a pump house on the right, and keep to the stream and ponds which are a few yards away on the right. Continue past a pond which has been created by a dam. Twenty yards beyond the dam, ignore a track on the left. In a further 30 yards, at a fork, go to the left on the gently ascending track. Continue ahead to another fork. Take the left hand ascending one. (The right hand one goes down to the stream where a wooden bridge can be seen.) This leads to a gate and stile just above the overgrown ruins of a building which is on the right. Go through and immediately turn right. Walk with a small wood on the right for a few yards and descend to a gate. Go through and so back to the stream.

Follow the stream for a further ½ mile. Just beyond a small lake, there is a definite track on the right. Do not follow this, but continue ahead and, where the valley sweeps round to the right, bear left through the wood.

Pass through a gate with a bridleway sign into a clearing and continue along a definite track with a wood on the right. In a short distance the path passes through woodland to a gateway. Go through into a field and bear left and ascend to a wall. Turn right and follow the wall to pass 2 modern barns. Do not go through the gate into the yard of the barns, but continue alongside the wall to the first gate on the left. Go through to the road and turn right to descend into Caudle Green.

CRANHAM COMMON AND SHEEPSCOMBE

A varied ramble with woodland and high ridges giving good distance views.
Map OS 163 in the 1:50,000 series.
Starting point grid reference 893131 – near the village of Cranham.
Distance 5½ miles.

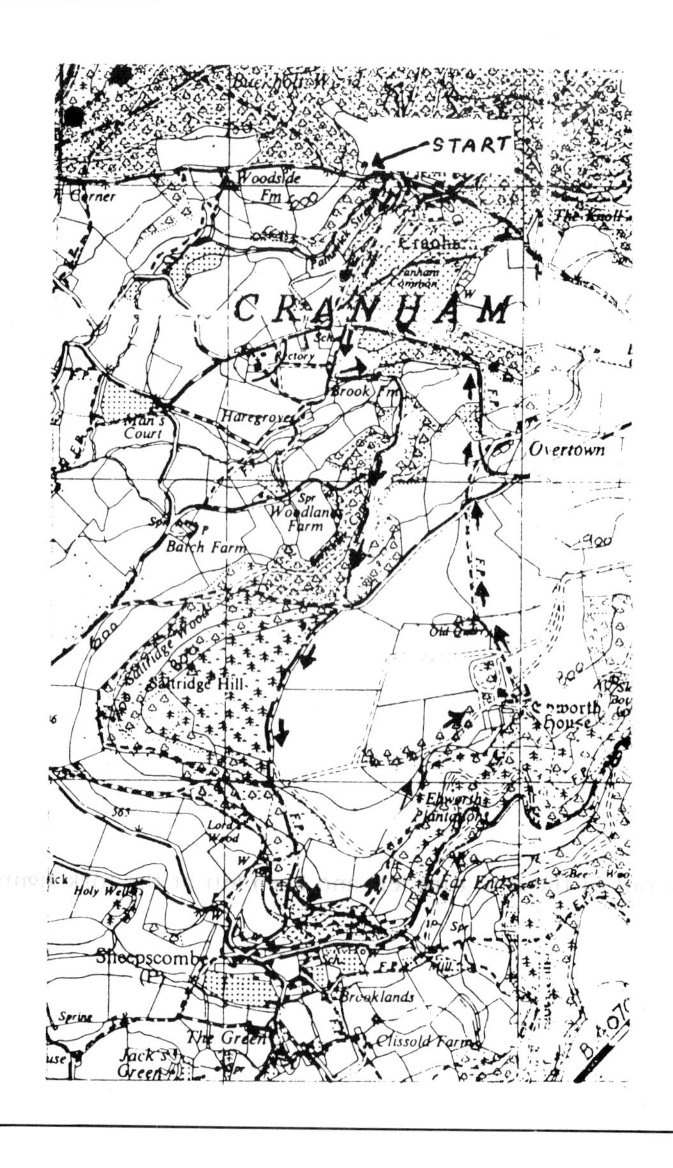

To get to the starting point from Cheltenham, go south on the A46: the Stroud road. In approximately 6 miles, pass over the A417 and continue for another 2½ miles. In a few yards past the entrance to Prinknash Abbey which is on the right, turn left, signposted Cranham 1 mile. In 100 yards at a fork, bear right and in a little over ½ mile, there is a parking place on the left in Buckholt Wood. This is the start of the ramble.

Go down the hill into Cranham village. At the bottom of the descent, cross the tiny Painswick stream. Fifty yards beyond the stream turn right. At the Black Horse Inn turn right and follow the sandy track. When the track forks, do not follow the right hand green track, but continue up the sandy track to the road.

Go straight ahead along the road. Go over the cross roads up the sandy track and pass to the left of some houses.

In 300 yards, the track turns left down to a farm. Go through a bridle gate to the left of the farm buildings and immediately beyond them, descend to the right to a stream. Do not go through the gate straight ahead, but turn right. Ascend for a few yards and go through a gate which leads to a sunken overgrown track. Continue up this track through the wood. At a point where there is a junction of tracks take the left hand ascending one and continue along this to a boundary wall nearly at the top of the ascent.

Follow this wall to the right to a facing gate. Do not go through this gate, but follow a path to the right of it through a gate-way. In about 30 yards, pass the gate which is on the left. In a further 10 yards, bear right down through the wood.

At a T-junction with another track turn left and continue descending through the wood. On coming to other tracks, keep bearing left. At a definite farm track continue ahead and follow it down to the road. Turn right to get to the Inn in Sheepscombe.

From the Inn, return along the road just traversed. (i.e. on coming out of the Inn, turn left and keep left at the fork signposted Sheepscombe Far End). In about 200 yards at Elm Cottage, take a track on the left of the road.

This leads in about 180 yards to a definite farm road. Cross this and go up the narrow ascending path opposite to a gate and stile. Go over and follow the hedge and fence which is on the right until a stile and gate are reached with a footpath waymark and a sign 'Workmans Wood – A National Nature Reserve'. Go into the wood and follow the footpath to a very definite wide track. Cross it immediately and go up the diagonal ascending path opposite with a waymark sign. Follow this path to another definite wide track which follow straight ahead. Follow this track until the main part of the track makes a loop to the right. Here take the ascending path on the left. This leads to a farm road where there is a notice 'A National Nature Reserve'.

Turn left, follow the road round to the right through the farm buildings and go through a farm gate. Ascend the track to go through another gate on to a farm road.

Turn left for about 30 yards, to a gate. Do not go through the gate but turn right up the field and follow the wall which is on the left to a stile. Go over the stile and walk along a path with a wood on the right and a wall on the left and go over a stile into a steeply banked open field.

Follow the bank veering right in a northerly direction and pass to the left of a clump of trees. This leads to a stile which is to the right of the corner of the field. The buildings of Overton will be seen below away on the right. Go towards the buildings and pass through a kissing gate. Descend left keeping close to the hedge on the right. This is immediately below the buildings. In about 150 yards look out for a way through the hedge which passes over a tiny stream which has been bridged. Make for the wicket gate seen ahead. Pass through and bear left and descend with the hedge now on the left. At the bottom of the descent go up the green track ahead which in a few yards ascends to a gate. Pass through into the wood. Follow the definite track until it emerges into the open common. Continue in the same direction to some cross paths. Here take the descending path to the left to the road.

Turn right. At a fork, take the sandy track to the left. This leads to the Black Horse Inn. Turn left down to the main road. Turn left and continue to the Buckholt Wood and the beginning and end of the walk.

RAMBLE 20

SHEEPSCOMBE, DOWNSWOOD, NORTH BANK, SNOWS FARM, TIMBERCOMBE COTTAGE, DILLAY

An exciting walk with remote valleys and fine hillside views.
Map OS 163 and 162 in the 1:50,000 series.
Starting point grid reference 891104 – the Butcher's Arms Inn in the village of Sheepscombe.
Distance 6 miles.

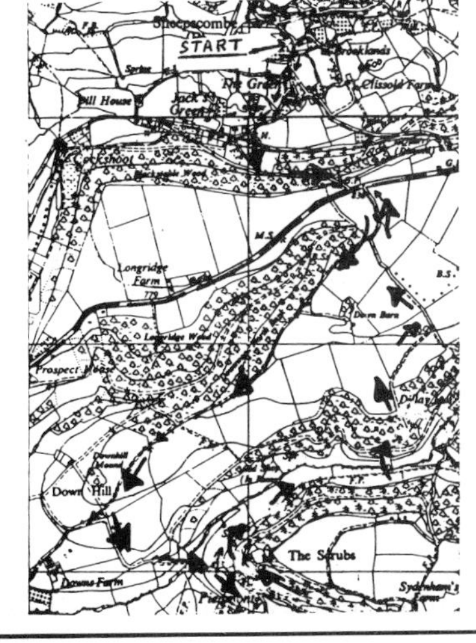

To get to Sheepscombe from Cheltenham, take the road to Birdlip. From Birdlip, take the B4070. In about 2¾ miles, pass the Fostons Ash Inn. In a further mile – at the cross roads – go right and continue to the Butcher's Arms Inn. This is the start of the walk.

Go down the descending road opposite the Butcher's Arms Inn. Pass the telephone kiosk and the Parish Hall which are on the left and continue past the church, also on the left, to a T-junction with another road. Immediately across this road is a narrow track leading uphill for about 200 yards to a stile. Pass over the stile to another track inside the wood. Turn left here and continue to the road. At the road, turn left and in 50 yards turn right. In about 300 yards, at a junction, continue ahead to pass on the left of a scrap yard. The track at first is through a wood then emerges into open country. Carry on to a notice 'No Through Road. Last Turning Point'. Here take the sharp left hand turn. A little further on pass through the gate with a notice 'Snows Farm'.

Proceed past the cottage and through another gate with a stile. Continue a few yards to a further gate with a stile to the right. Go over and bear left to descend to a stream. Pass over the stream and over the facing stile. Ascend the hill with the hedge, fence and wall on the left to reach a gate giving access to woodland. Enter the wood and go directly ahead without deviating from the narrow, but well-defined footpath which passes in front of two stone houses. About 50 yards beyond the second house, make a sharp left turn and ascend to a junction of tracks with a house immediately above a tarred road. Take the descending track to the left and, in about 180 yards at a fork, take the left descending track. At the end of the track, leave the wood through a gate.

Immediately turn right to follow the edge of the wood round the hillside. Where the upper and lower woods seem to merge, pass through a facing barbed wire fence to enter more woodland. Continue in the same direction, although fallen trees make it difficult to follow the indefinite path. Emerging from the wood into an open field, continue along the hillside in roughly the same direction with the stream at the bottom about 80 yards away, and a wood close on the right. Pass through some brushwood into another field, keeping the same direction for about 200 yards before descending gradually to the left to a gate in the corner of the field. Dillay can be seen on the opposite side of the valley.

Pass through a gate into a green track; turn left to Timbercombe Cottage. At this remote cottage, there is a lady of considerable character with whom we had a most interesting conversation. She had a wide experience and gave us many facets of the local scene and of the history of the area. She is Ms Rosie Bannon, and she said that some people in the area made comments associating her with the Rosie of 'Cider with Rosie'. This however was not confirmed by Ms Bannon, and her Irish lilt made the association very unlikely.

Go up the narrow path to the right of the cottage and immediately behind the cottage (within 20 yards) go over the stile on the left into a field. Descend into the valley. In less than 200 yards, at a waymark, cross over the fence and stepping-stones on the left and follow the fence on the left up to a cottage called Dillay. (There is an application to replace the stepping-stones with a bridge.) Follow the track to the left of the cottage up through a wood and into an open field. Continue ahead along a still definite track to pass to the right of a new farmhouse and to a T-junction. Here continue along the main track by turning right. In 300 yards, at the road, turn left.

In about 50 yards, leave the road to go down the track on the right. In about 450 yards, go over the stile on the right and descend the track into Sheepscombe.

RAMBLE 21

RANDWICK near to STROUD

A woodland walk
Distance 4 miles
Map OS 162 in the 1/50,000 series
Starting point grid reference 827067 village of Randwick

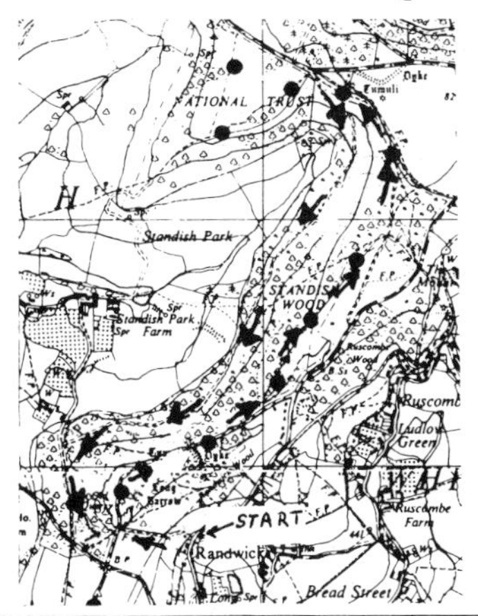

From just opposite the church in Randwick ascend the path at right angles to the road (waymarked yellow dot). Just after entering trees (Do not continue on the definite track ahead) you will see a 3 rail fence about 6 feet long with a gap/stile on the right. Go through this into a field and turn right. Ascend the field witha wood and fence on the right to a stile. Go over the stile to a track. Turn right and follow the Cotswold Way signs (White spot) through Standish Wood for 1½ miles to a car park. Grid reference 832086.

Turn around and walk back 100 yards to a junction of 3 tracks. Take the middle track and walk ahead keeping just within the western edge of Standish Wood. Keep on the good track (Ignoring a secondary path on the right after about ¾ mile) until a good farm road is reached. Turn left and in a few yards bear left up the track running in the same general direction as the road.

In 400 yards, by a large stone, turn left for 10 yards and then right to the facing stile by the wood edge. Keep the wood and fence on the left as you descend the field. At the bottom of the field pass through the 3 rail fence and gap/stile (This is the one passed through at the beginning of the walk) and descend to the church at Randwick.

RAMBLE 22

DANEWAY near SAPPERTON
(Sapperton is just over 5 miles west of Cirencester)

An interesting walk with woodland and the Thames Severn disused canal and the River Frome.
Distance 2½ miles
Map OS in the 1/50,000 series
Starting point grid reference 939034 Hamlet of Daneway

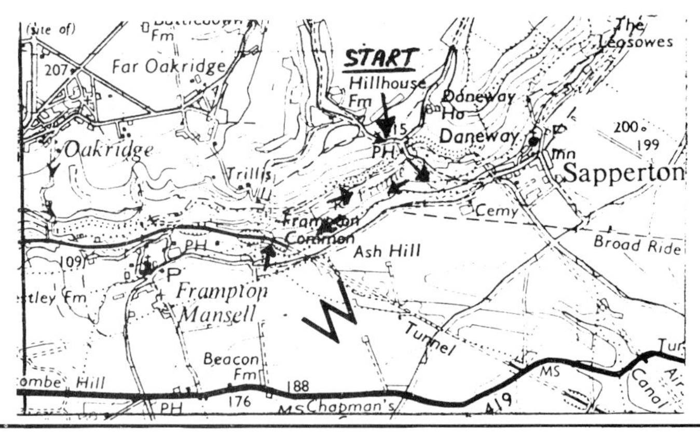

From the Daneway Inn pass over the River Frome Bridge. In a further 400 yards leave the road to take the track on the right as it cuts back. Carry on along the definite track for nearly a mile over Sapperton Common. Pass to the left of a circular on plan brick ventilating shaft. In 140 yards the road is reached. Turn right; go along the road for a short distance to a point where the road sweeps to the right. At this point there is a public footpath sign on the right and a farm track on the left to Beacon Farm.

Go along the footpath on the right into the wood which descends to the railway. Cross the track but take care as the line is still in use. Continue ahead for a short distance to a firm bridleway running to the left with a stone retaining wall on its left; proceed along this bridleway to another railway crossing. Do not go over this crossing but follow the track downhill to a small group of buildings.

Turn right here to reach the derelict canal and then follow to the right along the towpath of the canal. Continue along the towpath, pass under the brick built arched bridge dated 1784 to a wooden bridge set across a former lock. Cross the bridge and then walk on with the canal to the right until the path reaches the road opposite the Daneway Inn.

RAMBLE 23

EDGEWORTH, VALLEY FARM and RIVER FROME.

A charming hamlet, an interesting farm, a pleasant river walk a country of which one never tires.
Map OS 163 in the 1/50,000 series.
Starting point grid reference 948059 hamlet of Edgeworth.
Distance 5 miles

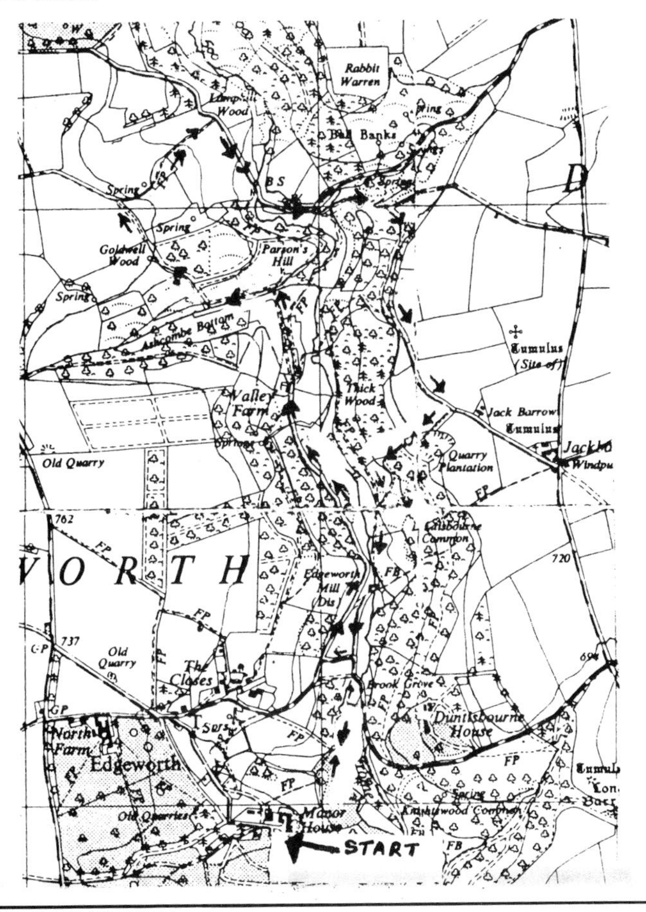

To get to Edgeworth go as follows;-
From Cirencester:
Go out on the A417 (T) northwards towards Birdlip. In about 1½ miles take a road on the left to Daglingworth. In Daglingworth continue westwards through the village to a fork. Bear right along the minor road. At the T-junction turn left and continue to and over the cross roads to Edgeworth.

From Cheltenham:
Take the A40(T). On leaving the town at a fork with traffic lights go right along A435. In three miles pass over the cross roads known as Seven Springs. In 1½ miles take the road on the right signposted Elkstone. Pass through Elkstone to the main road A417(T). Cross and continue through Winstone. In a further 2 miles take a road on the right to Edgeworth.
This is the start of the ramble.

Go past the church towards the manor house. Just before the Manor gates take a track on the right. It gives the impression of being private ground but it is a public right of way. This leads to a bridge. On the other side go up the track to the road. Turn left down the hill and cross the stream.

At the second left hand bend on the hill turn right, signposted Valley Farm, which is reached in ¾ mile. Here can be seen the outline of a very old stone oven. There is also an an amazing roof at the back of the farm.

Pass through Valley Farm leaving the farm buildings on the left and the valley on the right. Pass through one gate and then another and then to the left of a cattle shed and carry on to a facing fence. Go over the stile and turn left along a path. In just over 200 yards a gate is reached. The path is to the right, uphill, immediately before this gate. It was cleared by a party of ramblers with the consent of the landowner. It is, however, NOT entirely free of obstruction. (The easier way is to go through the gate and then turn right up the hill with the wood on the right but, unfortunately, it is NOT the right of way.) At the top of the field pass into the next field.

About 2/3rds of the way up this field pass over, at the best accessible point into the field on the left. (If you took the easier trespass way you would have come to this point.)

Go ahead with the fence on your right, through a gate, and in 250 yards turn sharply right at a Y-junction. A conifer plantation will be on your left. In about 200 yards go through a gate into a field keeping a hedge on your right. Where the hedge turns at right angles to the right leave this corner and continue in the same line to a gate on to the road. Turn right along the road. In about 600 yards, at a left hand bend of the road, 100 yards beyond the house on your left, leave the road and go through a gate on the right. Bear left through this gate up a sunken track and through another gate for about 300 yards in all.

Where the track forks go to the right into the wood (away from the line of wooden pylons). In about ½ mile you emerge from the wood by a definite track. 100 yards before a house called Jack Barrow turn down a path on the right with a wall on your left, which in about 100 yards goes to the right of a quarry plantation. Continue descending but about 60 yards before the River Frome, turn left through a gate. Gradually descend to the river, bearing to the left to cross by the foot-bridge into the farm cottage yard and ascend to the road. Turn left and go straight ahead to the T–junction. Turn left along the road which crosses the river and ascends the hill. About 200 yards up the hill from the river turn right into the track passing through the Manor grounds up to the starting point by the church.

RAMBLE 24

PINSBURY PARK, RIVER FROME, SAPPERTON.

An interesting discovery ramble
Map OS 163 in the 1/50,000 series
Starting point grid reference 961043 Park Corner near Sapperton
Distance 4½ miles.

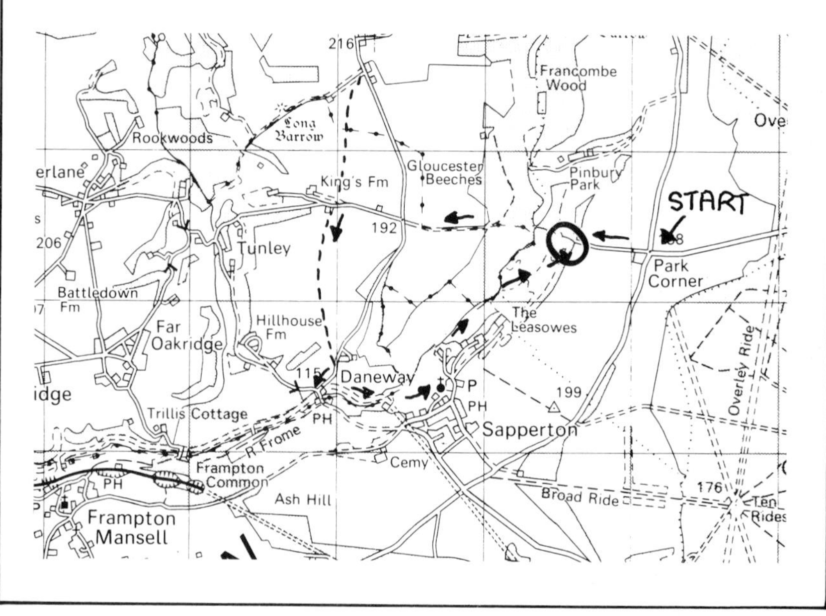

To get to the starting point;-
From Cirencester:
Go out on the A417(T) northwards towards Birdlip. In about 1½ miles take the road on the left to Daglingworth. Continue ahead past the road on the left to the church. Follow the road for another 200 yards to a fork. Bear left. In nearly 2 miles a cross road is reached.
This is the beginning of the ramble and you go straight ahead over the cross roads.
From Cheltenham:
Take the A40(T). On leaving the town at a fork with traffic lights, bear right along A435. In 3 miles pass over the cross roads called Seven Springs. In 1½ miles take the road on the right signposted Elkstone. Pass through Elkstone to the main road A417(T). Cross and continue ahead into Winstone. In Winstone turn left and go ahead for 3½ miles to the cross roads at Park Corner.
This is the beginning of the ramble.

Go along the road to the right passing some farm buildings. In 500 yards where the track bears left continue for 40 yards and then turn right-about to descend towards a gate; 20 yards before the gate turn left and descend through woodland. This leads to a ford across the River Frome. Ascend to the gate ahead (Avoid the wicket gate on the right) Go through the gate and in 20 yards take the ascending track on the right. Carry on without deviation for just over ½ mile to the road.

Go up the road opposite towards Kings House. In 550 yards immediately before a house on the left go up some rough steps and over a stile into a field. Follow the hedge on the right for 40 yards. Here leave the hedge and go towards the left hand of the spinney seen ahead. Going towards this spinney there will be a large open field on the right.

From the spinney follow the hedge which is on the right for about ¾ mile and then go over a stile into another field with a lot of scrub. Veer slightly left to pick up a track on the brow of the hill and follow this track as it descends to the right. Continue to the road opposite the entrance to Daneway House. Turn right. At the T-junction turn left.

Go past the Daneway Inn, cross the bridge, and immediatly take the footpath on the left signposted Sapperton.

Follow the green track on the raised bank with a disused canal on the left and a stream on the right. Cross a stile and continue along the track between brushwood and trees to pass to the left of a derelict cottage and so to the old canal tunnel. (The mason whose duty it was to keep the tunnel in repair lived at the cottage.)

The canal has now been filled in but it ran from Framilode on the Severn to Inglesham near Lechlade on the Thames. The engineer for this tunnel was the grandson of the famous Brunel.

Go left over the top of the tunnel to a stile/fence, cross it and then ascend diagonally right. The direction is towards the right hand of the church and a group of buildings seen ahead. At a fence cross a stile and follow the path ahead to go over a metalled track. At the road turn left into Sapperton.

Go to a point where there is a T-junction with the church on the left and the road to the Bell Inn on the right. Cross the T-junction . Go through the kissing gate, to the right of the telephone box, into the field.

Cross the pasture passing the electricity lines to a bridle gate (i.e. crossing it about equidistant from the wall on each side). Carry on across the next field in the same direction with a fence and hedge about 20 yards on the right. Here a gate leads into the next field, which must be crossed, with the fence still 20 yards on the right. Pass through the gate and some brushwood, and at the next gate enter a wood. The gate at the end of the wood leads to a piece of open ground with trees on each side. Continue ahead keeping close to the trees on the right. A fork is reached. Do not go down the left hand one which leads to a gate but follow the ascending one to the right. (This is the track which was walked in the reverse direction at the beginning of the walk.)

Follow this main track past farm buildings without deviation to Park Corner, the end and the beginning of the ramble.

RAMBLE 25

BOURTON–ON–THE–WATER and THE RISSINGTONS

Some typical Cotswold villages
Map 163 in the 1/50,000 series
Starting point grid reference 172202 Bourton-on-the-Water
Distance 6½ miles
This walk should be done in fine weather because after heavy rain mud becomes a difficult problem.

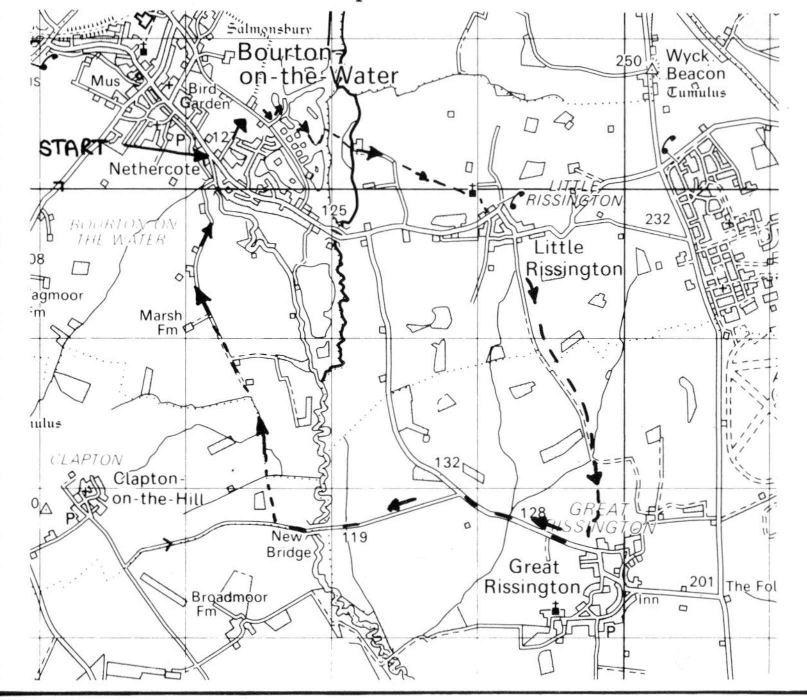

Start from the car park opposite the cricket ground at the south end of the village on the road to Little Rissington.

Turn right out of the car park. Take the first turn left sign-posted to walk with the playing field on the left. Continue ahead across a field with a hedge on the right. At the minor road turn right and in 200 yards follow the road round to the left to a gate. Pass through and in 20 yards take a definite track on the right. There is now a quarry pond on each side. (Look out for heron and grebe)

At the end of the ponds follow round to the left. In 200 yards turn right across a tiny stream by a footbridge.

Bear half right across the field to a gate with a stile on the left. Go over the stile and continue ahead to the stream. Follow the stream to the right and go over two footbridges with the buildings of Rissington Mill on the left. Go ahead to the road. Turn right.

In about 200 yards where the road bends sharply to the right go through a gate on the left. Go half right across the field and make for the middle point of the facing hedge. Go through, turn half left and ascend to the top righthand corner of this field.

Go over the stile/fence and then follow the hedge on the right round the field making for the church seen ahead. About 20 yards before the churchyard wall go through the wicket gate on the right. With the church on the left follow the footpath through to the church drive. Turn right to the road. Turn left through Little Rissington following the road as it makes a strong right turn.

Continue to the cross roads. Go over and down the sign-posted bridleway opposite with a house called Badgers Bank on the right.

Carry on for 1 mile through 4 gates. The fourth gate is arrived at after a descent through a field with a hedge on the right. After passing through this fourth gate follow the hedge which is on the right and go through the facing gate. Continue with the hedge still on the right over a field to a wicket gate on the right. Go through. In a few yards turn left through a gate and go over a hedge on the right. Make for the farm buildings (possibly deep mud at this point). Get on the farm track to the right of these buildings and continue to the road.

Turn right thus avoiding Great Rissington. In¾ mile take the first road on the left. In another ¾ mile pass over the River Windrush at New Bridge. In a further 300 yards turn right along a bridleway. Go ahead over the field keeping parallel to the hedge and trees on the left so as to arrive at a gate on the opposite side of the field. Pass through and go ahead in the same direction along a fairly definite track to arrive at a hedge. Continue in the same direction with this hedgeon the right. Pass through a gate into the next field and carry on to another gate to enter a small field preceding a farm.